kisses *of* sunshine

for teachers

Other Books in the Kisses of Sunshine Series

Kisses of Sunshine for Grandmas
by Carol Kent and Gracie Malone
Kisses of Sunshine for Moms
by Carol Kent and Ellie Kay
Kisses of Sunshine for Sisters
by Carol Kent
Kisses of Sunshine for Women
by Carol Kent and Thelma Wells

carol kent . vicki caruana

kisses *of* sunshine

for teachers

ZONDERVAN™

GRAND RAPIDS, MICHIGAN 49530 USA

Kisses of Sunshine for Teachers
Copyright © 2005 by Speak Up, Inc., and Vicki Caruana

Requests for information should be addressed to:

Zondervan, *Grand Rapids, Michigan 49530*

Library of Congress Cataloging-in-Publication Data

Kisses of sunshine for teachers / Carol Kent, general editor; Vicki Caruana,
    editor.
        p. cm.
    ISBN-10: 0-310-24767-5
    ISBN-13: 978-0-310-24767-8
    1. Teachers—Religious life—Anecdotes. I. Kent, Carol, 1947–
II. Caruana, Vicki.
BV4596.T43K58 2005
242'.68—dc22   2003018891

This edition printed on acid-free paper.

Published in association with the literary agency of Alive Communications, Inc., 7680 Goddard Street, Suite 200, Colorado Springs, CO 80920.

Interior design by Tracey Walker

Printed in the United States of America

---

05 06 07 08 09 10 11 12 /❖ DCI/ 10 9 8 7 6 5 4 3 2 1

contents

introduction

This *Kisses of Sunshine* series of five books — one each for teachers, moms, sisters, grandmas, and women — has lighthearted, uplifting, often humorous stories meant to bring a sunburst of joy to your life — as you remember that God loves you. Vicki Caruana has joined me in putting these stories together, and our purpose is simply to let God's love so warm and fill you that you become warmth, light, and love to the people around you.

This book in the series is for all women who teach. You might be an educator in an elementary school, a middle school, or a high school, or you may be a homeschool mom. *Kisses of Sunshine for Teachers* is also for Sunday school teachers, music and creative arts teachers. Actually, if you are a woman who is alive and breathing, you are no doubt teaching someone — even if it isn't in an "official" capacity.

As a classroom teacher for seven years, I soon discovered the power of stories to capture the hearts and minds of my students. This book is filled with true stories that will make you laugh out loud, renew your passion, and demonstrate practical how-to's that will make you a better teacher. It will also give you inspiration and momentum for your current teaching assignment.

Vicki Caruana is trademarked as "America's Teacher," and you may already know she's the author of *Apples & Chalkdust*, a book of inspiring stories for teachers that has sold more than

600,000 copies. (That's a lot!) She's witty, wise, and filled with down-to-earth advice for teachers. She speaks nationally at conventions and conferences for homeschoolers and other educators. Her heart for people who teach is obvious in everything she does. I wish I had known her before I became a teacher because I would have been better prepared for the task at hand.

Beware! Once you pick up this book and start reading, you'll find it hard to put down. But this is also a book people can read "on the run" — and teachers are usually running to the next assignment.

Vicki and I want to thank our editor at Zondervan, Sandra Vander Zicht, for being our encourager as we completed the gathering and writing of stories. Her vision for this project was unwavering, and it made us feel supported and appreciated.

As the general editor of this book, it was my delight to contact many of the best educators who have crossed my path and ask if they had any "teacher stories" to share. Every time I opened my email and read another vignette, I realized this book was going to be better than I ever imagined. Teachers were authentic enough to tell about their challenges, their mistakes, their hilarious classroom memories, their failures, their choices — good and bad — and their dreams for what teaching can become when we do it right. You are my heroes, my mentors, and my cheerleaders! I hope this book reminds you of why you do what you do. Bravo to all of you who teach!

— CAROL KENT, GENERAL EDITOR

the cowboy, the princess, and superman

Carol Kent

. . . .

Teachers are not born; they are made. . . .
A good teacher is first of all teachable.

HENRIETTA MEARS

*a*few months after our marriage, my husband and I moved to Grand Rapids, Michigan, where Gene enrolled in graduate classes. Our move was in January and there didn't appear to be any teaching positions available in my subject areas. However, there was a kindergarten class that had an opening — and the school system was so desperate for a teacher, they asked me to join the faculty even though my credentials were in secondary education.

My first day was a blur of activity — parents taking pictures, children crying, keeping order, setting up routines, enforcing nap time, and trying to teach something of value that would validate my worth as a paid teacher. That day I also discovered why some educators *choose* to teach kindergarten. I had a room filled with dynamic, charming personalities who suddenly found me in the center of their world.

Jeremy was dressed in jeans, a plaid shirt, red scarf, cowboy boots, and a mini-Stetson. He ambled up to me and said, "Hi, pardner! I'm here to protect you and to defend our class against any enemies. Let me know if I can be of service." (I liked this charming young man from the Wild West!)

Susan was dressed in a white eyelet dress that looked more appropriate for church than for school. On her head she proudly wore a plastic crown. As I passed by her desk, she gazed up and said, "My daddy says I'm a princess. Do you think I'm a princess, too?" With a smile, I nodded in agreement.

As I rounded the corner of the next row, there was Peter. He was wearing blue jeans, but instead of a shirt, he wore the pajama top from a Superman outfit, complete with a red cape that dangled precariously from Velcro on the tops of his shoulders. His eyes twinkled as he said, "If you need me, I'm here!" I chuckled out loud and verbalized my appreciation for his offer.

A couple of weeks into my adventure with the kindergartners, I came into the classroom with a heavy heart. That morning I had had "words" with my husband and felt unjustly criticized. We'd had the classic newlywed fight over how I squeezed the toothpaste tube. Even though it was a small issue, my feelings were hurt.

Princess Susan walked up to my desk. She was in casual clothes that day, but her prized crown was still on top of her golden locks. Gazing up at me seriously, she asked, "Are you sad today, Teacher?"

"A little," I responded honestly.

"Well," she said, putting her hands on her hips, "you'll just have to get over that because I think you are the best teacher in the world and I love you very much!" With that, she threw her arms around me and placed a kiss on my cheek.

Later in the day I watched two of my students settle a disagreement amicably and turn back into "best buddies" during recess. They didn't hold grudges and they joyfully picked up where they left off in their relationship. I felt a little silly for continuing to hold a grudge against my husband over a tube of toothpaste. It was time to let go of my petty resentment.

I gazed at the class—Cowboy Jeremy, Superman Peter, and the rest of my remarkable five-year-old charges. They were teaching me everything I needed to know about facing daily challenges and being a successful teacher: forgive quickly, love unconditionally, visualize your future (whether it's to be a cowboy, a princess, or Superman), live each day with gusto, and take frequent naps. It's a winning combination—and I'm still benefiting from their positive examples today.

. . . .

Let the wise listen and add to their learning.

PROVERBS 1:5

supply and demand

Vicki Caruana

....

If you were reimbursed for teaching materials, you'd be rich.

KIMBERLY CHAMBERS

*E*ach school year has its own ebb and flow. In my experience, the flow turns into a slow trickle sometime around the end of February. Not only does our enthusiasm wane, so do our supplies! My husband is still mystified that there isn't some secret supply closet for teachers to go to when they run out of copy paper, pencils, crayons, construction paper, chalk or dry erase markers, legal pads, index cards, envelopes, and anything else you might find in a school — including toilet paper!

At the end of each school year, I tried desperately to project (within my allotted budget, that is) what supplies I would need to carry us through the next school year. Everything — down to paper clips and Scotch tape — had to be itemized in the budget. When the supplies came in at the beginning of the year (if they all came in), we carefully distributed the appropriate number of supplies to each teacher. Since teachers are very territorial by nature, any mistake in distribution, no matter how slight, could result in frustration, lost items, and mayhem!

I remember one time when I ended up with one more box of staples than I ordered. As a beginning teacher, I did not realize the severe ramifications of such an oversight. I was happily organizing my supplies in my classroom when I heard a not-so-friendly "Ah-hem!" from behind. I turned to see one of my colleagues, her supply invoice and red pen in one hand and the other extended in expectation.

"I think you have something that belongs to me," she snarled.

"I don't think so," I said with complete ignorance. Whoever said ignorance was bliss?

"Let me see your invoice," she said, her extended hand now grasping in desperation.

"Certainly," I said. I handed her my invoice and continued to stack my supplies.

"Aha!" she exclaimed in triumph. "If my calculations are correct, and I'm sure they are, you've stacked one too many boxes of staples, young lady."

I guess my inexperience combined with my charming personality didn't matter. I counted the staples for myself and discovered, much to my dismay, that I did indeed have one box too many. I removed the box from the neatly organized shelf and handed it over gingerly, afraid my hand was going to be slapped.

"I'm sorry. I just assumed the supplies had been correctly distributed," I said with complete humility.

"Next time make sure you only have what you ordered and not someone else's property!" the teacher said and stormed out of my classroom.

I looked at the invoice in my hand and then at my supply cabinet. I started the day with eight boxes of staples and a concern they wouldn't be enough. Now I had only seven *and* an angry new colleague.

I don't think anyone has ever explained the principle of supply and demand to educators. Teachers' school supplies never seem to meet their demands. We are so concerned with whether our physical needs are met that often we put those concerns above all else. But while our supplies may seem to come from the district warehouse, ultimately we have what we have because God has given it to us. When your supplies dwindle and you are scrambling to make do with what's left, know that God has already equipped you perfectly for the very work he has prepared for your hands — given a box of staples more or less.

. . . .

And my God will meet all your needs
according to his glorious riches in Christ Jesus.

PHILIPPIANS 4:19

frankie and mr. b

Janet Fleck

....

The direction in which education starts a man
will determine his future life.

PLATO

*a*t the age of twenty-four, I taught second grade at a small rural school in Michigan. Seven-year-old Frankie was one of my students. Everything about him conveyed a "poor lost boy" look: disheveled hair, grungy fingernails, smudged face, stained plaid pajama top worn as a shirt over threadbare pants, and scuffed, worn tennis shoes.

Each day I called small groups of children to sit around a kidney-shaped table and take turns reading out loud. When it was Frankie's turn, he laid his head on the table, covered it with his arms, and refused to read. I didn't force him to read that day, or the next day, or the day after that. Finally I pulled him aside and asked, "Frankie, don't you *want* to learn to read?"

In a try-and-make-me tone, Frankie said, "I don't need to know how to read. My dad don't know how to read."

Realizing this was more than a teacher-student issue, I looked for a telephone number to call the family. When I could not find one, I made a home visit.

On a Friday after school, I drove down a long, narrow dirt road to a place you wouldn't expect to find a house. I saw the neglected, beat-up residence as soon as I turned onto the gravel driveway.

Frankie answered my knock and took me to meet his dad. Mr. B was tall and thin, with a missing front tooth and a short, scruffy beard. He wore a plaid flannel shirt. He stared at me through sad eyes. I felt instant compassion for this man who was only in his mid-twenties and who had a beaten-by-life expression.

"Mr. B, Frankie tells me he doesn't need to know how to read because you don't know how to read. Is that true?" I paused before adding, "If it is true, I'd like to offer you some help."

He paused to take in the question and to evaluate my sincerity. Slowly he answered, "It's true. I dunno how to read or write, and my mom and dad dunno how either."

After we talked a while, I got up my courage and extended an invitation. "You are welcome to come to the Adult Basic Education classes that I teach two evenings a week in Brighton." I assured him, "You won't be the only adult there who can't read or write."

With unexpected humility, Mr. B admitted that he needed to learn to read so he could fill out job applications, get a job, and give Frankie a better life. But Mr. B was skeptical. He told me he couldn't learn to read at Frankie's age, so he couldn't understand why it would be different now.

As he walked me to the door, I looked him in the eyes and challenged him: "Mr. B, what you choose to do about your own education will determine Frankie's future." Then I said goodbye and made my way out the door.

Much to my surprise, Mr. B came to the next adult education class and brought his mother, father, and a cousin with him. I quickly discovered that, like Frankie, they could not connect the sound-symbol relationships of the letters in words. They were classic examples of people who needed specific, focused instruction to learn to read.

Over the next few weeks and months, with intense, direct instruction, Mr. B learned to read and write. Every week, as his reading and writing skills improved, so did his confidence. Frankie's enthusiasm for reading grew stronger each week, too. In fact, Frankie became an enthusiastic reader. One day he proudly proclaimed, "My dad helped me with my reading. We read my book together."

By the end of the year, not only had Mr. B's confidence improved, he had also reached a personal goal. He was reading at a fifth grade level — well enough to fill out job applications. Frankie was reading at his grade level, too.

On the last night of the adult education class, Mr. B, his mother, father, cousin, and I left the building together. With hope-filled eyes, Mr. B said, "Thank you for teaching us to read and write and for helping me to help my son."

As Frankie's family left the parking lot, I felt a deep sense of satisfaction — the kind that comes from knowing you saw a need, took a risk, and reaped a reward. It was a day I loved being a teacher.

. . . .

But what happens when we live God's way? He brings gifts into our lives, much the same way that fruit appears in an orchard — things like affection for others, exuberance about life, serenity. We develop a willingness to stick with things, a sense of compassion in the heart, and a conviction that a basic holiness permeates things and people. We find ourselves involved in loyal commitments, not needing to force our way in life, able to marshal and direct our energies wisely.

GALATIANS 5:22–23 MSG

take charge!

Vicki Caruana

. . . .

Never doubt in the dark what God told you in the light.

V. RAYMOND EDMAN

*I*nternships can be particularly intimidating situations. Unless you're blessed with a supervising teacher who goes out of his or her way to show you the ropes, you may end up feeling like part of one of your student's science experiments — one that went horribly wrong! Maybe it would help if student teachers were paid interns. But I suspect there is no amount of money that could erase the feelings of helplessness and inadequacy all student teachers feel.

My final student teaching assignment took place in a high school with a class of learning-disabled students. I was twenty-one and most of my students were nineteen. I knew right away that my greatest challenge would be maintaining my position of authority.

I remember entering the school and forcing my way through the crowd of more than two thousand teenagers prowling the main hallway like an ocean full of piranhas. I felt sure I'd be eaten alive by the end of the first week.

Mrs. Randall, my supervising teacher, graciously welcomed me to the classroom and led me to a small desk on the opposite side of the room.

"The kids will be here in about ten minutes," she said. "I believe in jumping right in, so as soon as the bell rings, you're on!"

My stomach gurgled in protest. I had no idea what to expect or what to do about whatever was to happen next. Quickly I arranged my materials and then stood at the front of the room scanning the board for a piece of chalk.

The bell rang. I heard the shuffling of feet behind me and also what sounded like catcalls. What was this — a construction site? I turned around to find a class full of seventeen- to nineteen-year-old boys. I had no clue how to break the ice. Fear cornered me.

As frantic thoughts of what I should do or say spun through my head, I turned just in time to see a paper airplane soaring directly at my face. Without thinking I caught the airplane in mid-flight and said, "Incoming!"

The students' critical stares immediately turned to grins of acceptance. With one confident move, I had captured their attention. Now they were wondering what I'd do next. I relaxed and began to teach.

Students can smell weak leadership like a wild animal can smell fear. Even when you walk into a situation for which you feel ill-equipped, you need to take charge. Put your confidence in God and he will lay your fears to rest and put your students at ease.

. . . .

"For I am the Lord, your God, who takes hold of your right hand and says to you, Do not fear; I will help you."

ISAIAH 41:13

the contest

Cathy Gallagher

. . . .

Truth is the beginning of every good thing, both in heaven and on earth; and he who would be blessed and happy should be from the first a partaker of truth, for then he can be trusted.

Plato

*J*n my senior year of high school I took a speech class with Mrs. Smith. At the end of the semester she arranged a contest to give us experience speaking before an audience. Three judges would select first place, second place, and third place winners who would receive United States savings bonds as prizes.

All twenty-five of us had worked hard to perfect our five-minute talks on "What Democracy Means to Me." We had practiced. Mrs. Smith had coached us, giving each of us her best. Even so, we were nervous about delivering our speeches to an audience of parents and classmates.

That night, one presentation stood out. My silent plea as I listened to Delores's speech was: *Oh, while I can never be that good, please let me not fall flat on my face!* I was sure Delores would be the first-place winner, and I knew she deserved it.

My name was called last. My mother squeezed my hand and whispered, "Good luck, honey," as I got up from my seat in the audience and approached the stage. When I finished, Mrs. Smith announced a break while the judges tallied the scores. Delores and I were standing together near the stage. The judges handed Mrs. Smith their results and, after studying them, she motioned for us to meet her backstage.

"Congratulations, Cathy, you've won first place, and Delores, you've won second place!" she said. I was surprised and elated. Delores was crushed. Then, speaking softly just to me, Mrs. Smith continued, "Cathy, you can handle what I'm going to say next. I must do this."

Tears were streaming down Delores's face. Mrs. Smith pulled out the judges' scores and said, "Cathy, you won because all three judges consistently ranked you number two. Delores, two judges ranked you number one, but the third judge ranked you number three. When the scores were tallied, Cathy's score was highest. Because her scores were consistent, she won first place."

I was stunned. My thoughts were swirling. *I don't get it! I won first place because I was consistent, not because I was the best?* It was more than I could grasp at age seventeen.

Feeling undeserving, but seeing no other choices, I did manage to walk onto the stage, smile, and accept the first-place award, but my win was bittersweet. How I wish it had occurred to me to swap places with Delores — allowing her to receive the first-place award that even I felt she deserved!

Years later, I understand the tough choice Mrs. Smith had to make about whether or not to share the judges' scores with us. She had to choose between keeping my heart intact or building up Delores's broken heart. She knew our hopes, our dreams, our levels of self-confidence, and the lessons we could learn from hearing the truth. She saw the bigger picture. She made the best decision she could make in that moment.

At the time, my teacher's comments stunned, angered, and confused me, but they did not devastate or diminish me for long. Looking back, I would have been more confused if Mrs. Smith had *not* shared the judges' scores because I would never have understood why I won. In trusting me enough to handle the truth, Mrs. Smith taught me that truth and consistency count.

. . . .

And you will know the truth, and the truth will set you free.

JOHN 8:32 NLT

open house

Vicki Caruana

· ·

Do the thing you believe in. Do the best you can in the place where you are and be kind.

SCOTT NEARING

Open House Night is always nerve-racking. It doesn't seem to matter how many times you prepare for this night, it always creates a wave of panic before the first parents walk in. Even more than the children's work is on display; *you* feel on display.

One year I spent all week pulling my sixth grade classroom together for the "big show." I mounted student work on color-coordinated construction paper. I organized every nook and cranny in the room. I even scrubbed the desktops with awful-smelling abrasive cleanser until they shone!

On the night of the open house the room was packed—standing room only. It's always cute to see parents try to squeeze into the small student chairs. But I'd learned that some of their squirming had nothing to do with the bottom-pinching chairs and more to do with their own recollection of what school is like. Those of us who loved school became teachers. That meant that many of the parents sitting in my classroom this night did not have pleasant memories of school. Schools have a smell to them — a mixture of cleaning fluid, finger paint, and chalk and — oh, yes — something cooking in the cafeteria. It all mingles together to make some of us smile and others bolt out the front door. I could tell my classroom was filled with the latter group.

After a simple introduction about myself and my goals as a teacher, I circulated in the crowd and handed out a scavenger hunt. The goal of this activity was to break the ice. Within minutes children and parents were navigating the room looking for things on their list. When at last everyone returned to their seats, I was met with relaxed, smiling faces. *Maybe this place isn't as bad as I remember it to be*, some seemed to be thinking. They reposed in their pint-sized chairs and uncrossed their arms. It was a good start to a great year.

Whether our extra effort goes unnoticed or is met with applause shouldn't change our motivation. Sometimes these efforts are successful and we please everyone. Other times we can do everything right and please no one. Our first desire must be to please God, and if we please men as a result, that's just icing on the cake.

Open House is a time to open yourself up to new opportunities. There are chances to build relationships and chances to reach and teach to the needs of your students. There are occasions for discovery and delight each and every day. Let your next Open House be the first night of the rest of the school year and make it a night to remember.

. . . .

Never let loyalty and kindness get away from you! Wear them like a necklace; write them deep within your heart. Then you will find favor with both God and people.

PROVERBS 3:3 – 4 NLT

a mighty clap

Melissa S. Sutter

· ·

Don't let your pride become inflated —
you may have to swallow it someday.

14,000 QUIPS & QUOTES

"Mrs. Sutter, you would be lucky to do ten push-ups," Kyle said with a smirk. The student issuing the challenge was a member of my blended class of eleventh and twelfth grade algebra students — and he was testing me.

"Lucky? That would just be a warm-up for me," I gushed with confidence. I mean, did this teen have any idea who I was? How could he say I would be lucky to do ten push-ups? I was in great shape. Hadn't he noticed my buff biceps? What was he thinking? What other high school teacher had recently placed in two arm wrestling competitions? The kid was crazy.

"Prove it," he challenged.

Eyebrows raised, I retorted, "I would prove it, but ten push-ups really aren't worth my time." Every ounce of me wanted to drop down and give him a hundred push-ups right then and right there. The competitive spirit in me began to rear its ugly head.

Kyle blurted out, "I knew you couldn't do it."

"It has nothing to do with my ability," I stated matter-of-factly. "It has everything to do with the inappropriateness of me showing off my great strength during an algebra class."

"That's all right, Mrs. Sutter. I wouldn't want to see you hurt yourself anyway," Kyle said.

I knew he was teasing. I knew I was too mature to be sucked into such an immature conversation. But I also knew I could do more push-ups than he could dream of doing! I wanted to ignore him. I wanted to set a good example. But I wanted to prove him wrong more. I could not resist.

"Not only will I do ten push-ups, Kyle, but I will clap between each one," I boasted, as I literally got into push-up position in front of my entire class.

After lowering my body to the floor the first time, I exploded upwards and made a mighty clap. Unfortunately for me, clapping between push-ups was harder than I remembered, and I quickly and forcefully smashed my forehead on the floor! In silence, I screamed "Ouch!" to myself as I gritted my teeth and not-so-gracefully finished the remaining nine push-ups — without claps.

Although my head hurt, I was feeling quite proud of myself for finishing well and playing off what could have been a truly humiliating experience. The students weren't saying anything, and I was quite sure they had not noticed the crushing blow to my forehead.

Feeling victorious, I raised myself from the floor and proudly faced my class. I will never forget the looks on my students' faces as they pointed to me in unison, laughing at what they described as a "red welt" on my forehead. The secret was out. My arrogance was gone. Pride destroyed, I had learned my lesson.

*When pride comes, then comes disgrace,
but with humility comes wisdom.*

PROVERBS 11:2

out of order

Vicki Caruana

One of my greatest desires was to teach in a brand-new school. A school where the classrooms were bright and airy, the desks were all the same size and shape, and where everything worked! As they say, be careful what you wish for . . .

New schools were popping up everywhere where we lived. New construction couldn't keep up with the population explosion. There was ample opportunity to transfer to one of these cutting-edge, technology-driven schools whose architecture boasted of its modern thinking and contemporary ways. The closest I ever got to teaching in one of these jewels was during summer school. But I wasn't the teacher, just a parent dropping off her children for a summer program for gifted students. I hung around while my children went to their classes, hoping to soak up the extravagances of this place of learning. I wanted to see for myself if the grass was indeed greener here.

This new school, one of many, was already overcrowded after just one year. Portable classrooms were scattered along its perimeter. The new landscaping was dying due to our ever-present drought (so I guess the grass wasn't greener after all), and nothing seemed to work as it was designed to work.

The clocks in each classroom were imprisoned by a cage, so no one would mess with them. However, neither did the custodian, and during daylight saving time they weren't changed. The windows, as many as there were, were not designed to be opened, and on the days when the air conditioning didn't work, we cursed that design. Finally, the thermostats in each classroom were also imprisoned by Plexiglas cages and inaccessible to anyone but the custodian. That would be fine if all the classrooms maintained the right temperature, but they did not.

There was a professionally decorated teachers' lounge, but it had only one telephone in it. The telephone did have five lines, but it still took me more than twenty minutes to get a line. I stood there with my finger poised over the blinking lights, waiting for one to go out. Obviously I wasn't the only one waiting for the phone because it took eight tries before my finger made contact. I felt like I was playing the arcade game Whack-a-Mole and wasn't very good at it.

The brand-new cafeteria was beautiful and spic-and-span. The lunchroom manager wanted to keep it that way. Hot lunches cooked from scratch were quickly replaced by hot dogs, hamburgers, and pizza ordered from a local pizzeria. Less clean up! Less nutritious food.

The final straw was the teachers' restroom. You needed a key. I retrieved the key only to discover the restroom was out of order! The other teachers' restroom, on the other side of the building, required a different key, and no one around seemed to know where that key was. I got in my car and drove home to take care of business.

It took that one day for me to appreciate my school. It may have been built in 1926, but I could change the clock when I needed to. I could open my windows on beautiful days. I could enjoy the native perennial plantings that have survived countless droughts since 1926. And I could use any bathroom I wanted — without needing a key! It took a lot less to make me happy than I thought it would. I guess you could call me a cheap date.

It's so easy to become discontented as a teacher. If you're struggling in a school that is less than perfect, consider it a testing of your faith and pray for God's peace and contentment. God may choose to move you, but he may decide to stay with you in your current school even if the walls are crumbling around you and everywhere you turn things are out of order.

I am not saying this because I am in need, for I have learned to be content whatever the circumstances. I know what it is to be in need, and I know what it is to have plenty. I have learned the secret of being content in any and every situation, whether well fed or hungry, whether living in plenty or in want.

PHILIPPIANS 4:11–12

worrywarts

Jennie Afman Dimkoff

Worry never accomplishes anything except wrinkles — which gives you another thing to worry about.

E. C. McKenzie

hat is that sound? I wondered. Looking up from my desk at the front of the crowded kindergarten classroom, I surveyed thirty little bodies stretched out on their mats in various poses of rest. I thought I had heard something, but all was quiet. *They're exhausted. It's no wonder that so many of them fall sound asleep when it's rest time each afternoon,* I thought.

The year was 1976. The place was a small, overcrowded, under-resourced K-12 public school in rural Louisiana, which was located down the highway from the Army base at Ft. Polk, where my husband was stationed. The days were long. My domain was a small mobile classroom filled with very young children, situated in the parking lot in front of the school. In that parish children started kindergarten at age four and attended classes all day, from 7:45 in the morning to 3:15 in the afternoon. Without the benefit of water or restroom facilities in our building, we took necessary bathroom breaks en masse several times a day, trudging approximately a city block to reach the nearest restroom, and then a bit farther to the playground. Keeping up with thirty children without the benefit of a teacher's aide left me exhausted by the end of each day.

But I loved them. With their piping little voices already seasoned with southern drawls, their winsome, often toothless grins and scraped knees, they were irresistible. On some days, I learned as much from them as they did from me.

I kept listening for the sound as I worried about my future. In three months, my husband's military commitment as a JAG officer would be completed, and we would be heading home to Michigan and an unknown future. Although he had applied for positions with several law firms, nothing looked promising. In that quiet classroom, my thoughts wandered: *Where will we live? Who will Graydon work for? Will he try to open his own law practice? Will I be able to get a job? Will we live in a house or an apartment?* Anxiety crowded in and left me sick to my stomach — again.

"You are such a worrywart, Jennie," my husband had said the night before when I expressed my panic to him. "In fact, I think you *love* to worry. Can't you just be patient and wait and see what God has for us? It won't do a bit of good to sit and make yourself sick with concern over something that may or may not happen. We can pray and plan, but then we have to leave it with the Lord. You just can't seem to do that, can you?"

Graydon's accusation had been gentle, but it left me frustrated. Bowing my head at my desk, I cried out to God, "Father, I can't seem to get beyond this uncertainty in my life. Please help me!"

Then I heard the strange sound again. In fact, the noise sounded like a whimper. I looked out over my classroom again, noticing this time that, although little Tracie Williams had curled herself into a small ball, her shoulders were shaking with quiet sobs.

Tiptoeing my way between the sleeping children, I made my way to the little girl. "Tracie," I whispered, "what's the matter, honey?"

Scrubbing tears from her eyes with one hand, she reached out to me with the other, her eyes a mirror of her distress. Enfolding her in my arms, I repeated my question. "Tracie, what in the world is the matter?"

Swallowing a sob, she drawled mournfully, "Teacher, my pierced ears are hurtin' me."

"They are?" I asked, instantly concerned. "Here, let's see. Perhaps you have an infection." I gently pushed back baby-fine, curly blonde hair to reveal both her ears and stared in surprised confusion at the little girl.

"Tracie," I said gently, lifting her chin to look her in her eyes, "honey, you don't *have* pierced ears."

The eyes that met mine welled up with tears. "I know, Teacher," she said woefully, "but I think I'm gonna be *getting* 'em pierced."

"Ah, so you're miserable on this beautiful day because of something that hasn't even happened yet." I stifled a rueful smile as thoughts of my own very recent behavior assailed me. "That seems just a little silly, doesn't it?" I gently rearranged her hair and added, "And that, Tracie Williams, would make you a worrywart."

"I don't want to be a *wart*," Tracie stated with emphasis.

"Me neither," I whispered, realizing God had used a little girl to reveal the foolishness of my own anxious heart. "Come and help me with a project at my desk for a little while, and that will get your mind off your ears."

That year my kindergarten student taught me a lesson for a lifetime. Worrying about anything before it happens is a terrible waste of energy!

* * *

Do not be anxious about anything, but in everything, by prayer and petition, with thanksgiving, present your requests to God.

PHILIPPIANS 4:6

survey says!

Vicki Caruana

. . . .

When we are flat on our backs there is no way to look but up.

ROGER W. BABSON

*O*ur school's professional library had more than stacks of books and educational journals in it — it had a coffee bar! For a while I was on the hunt for something — anything — that might improve my attitude in the classroom. I felt on the verge of burnout and scoured the journals for advice that might lighten my load. I found what I was looking for over coffee instead.

It had been a hard year. I changed positions within my school and the transition did not go as smoothly as expected. I went from teaching learning disabled students to teaching gifted learners. The problem was I did it after the school year had started. The students weren't happy. Their parents weren't happy. And by January, I wasn't happy.

That same year I experienced great loss during my first pregnancy. At twenty weeks, I lost our baby girl. Even after two weeks of recuperation at home I couldn't seem to muster the same enthusiasm for teaching that I once had. I lost the ability to find joy in my work — in my students and their accomplishments. As I look back, I realize I was spiraling down into depression.

For weeks my colleagues tiptoed around me, not quite sure what to say. Not only had I lost a child, I had lost my confidence as a teacher. This new position was much more work than I anticipated, and I just didn't have the emotional energy to put into it what was necessary. My lessons were lackluster. My thoughts were scattered. My countenance said to everyone what my words could not: *I'm alone. I'm scared. I don't want to be here anymore.*

I found that professional library to be a haven. It wasn't visited very often by other teachers, so in it I found solace and peace. I read through the journals and zeroed in on anything that talked about motivating students. I knew that I was the one who needed the motivating, but journals rarely cover what a teacher needs. Maybe I could find something to adapt to my situation.

One day while I sat with my hot cocoa–coffee concoction, a stranger waltzed in. He surveyed the journal stacks and shook his head in disappointment. "Nope. Your school doesn't have it either." I wasn't sure if he expected me to comment, so I just buried myself deeper into my current journal.

"Hey, smile!" He interrupted my pity party.

He obviously wasn't satisfied with my response — I didn't give him one — and sat down next to me.

"Sorry to butt in. My name is Don Elliot. I'm presenting the workshop today at your faculty meeting on stress on the job." His extended hand forced me out of my cocoon.

Stress workshop? I doubted his presentation would cover what ailed me. "Well, I guess I'll see you there," I said unenthusiastically.

"You look like you're busy. I'll leave you alone. But would you mind if I offered one piece of advice?"

I just looked at him and waited.

"First, never drink alone," he said and pointed to my coffee. When that didn't get a rise out of me, he turned serious and said, "Smile and the world smiles with you. Just fake it and eventually your emotions will catch up with you."

With that he turned and left me to my coffee to consider his words. *Fake it?* That's not something I saw anywhere in these journals. I doubted there was research to support it either.

The bell rang, signaling my last class of the day — the one I had the least energy for. Almost against my will I followed this stranger's advice. I walked into my classroom with a smile pasted onto my face. I took attendance with that smile. I passed out the test with that smile. I even called on a student with that smile. The funny thing is that by the end of those fifty minutes, that smile had without my notice become *my* smile. My smile dismissed the class and the smiles of my students beamed right back!

I didn't realize that when God said in James to "count it all joy," he didn't mean to wait until I felt like it.

* * *

Consider it pure joy . . . whenever you face trials of many kinds.

JAMES 1:2

snakes, snails, and
puppy dog tails

Cynthia Spell Humbert

. . . .

Who dares to teach must never cease to learn.

JOHN COTTON DANA

*I*t was Christian's premier day in the first grade. And at the ripe old age of seven, my son had his first big crush. He really knew how to pick the perfect girl, too — his teacher, Mrs. Jenny Emly, barely five feet tall, with a flawless peaches-and-cream complexion, darling smile, and beautiful brown hair.

As I listened to her plans for teaching our children that year, I was in a surreal state of confusion. I truly wanted to pay attention, but I kept looking at the beautiful young woman in front of these brand-new students. Turning to a friend, I whispered, "How old do you think she is?"

"I'm not sure," she replied, "but I heard she just finished college. I guess that would make her twenty-two or twenty-three."

Another mother chimed in, "The principal said she has only been married for a few weeks."

I started calculating the numbers to see if I was actually old enough to be her mother. The appalling answer fired through my mind, "Yes, Cynthia, if you had skipped college and started straight in on babies, she could be your daughter." I swallowed the hard knot in my throat and tried to concentrate on the words of enthusiasm pouring out of that lush, unwrinkled mouth.

As the school year progressed, Christian was so in love with Mrs. Emly that he lived in fear of disappointing her. He behaved so well for her that by the time school got out each day, he was overflowing with stored-up energy. He seemed to get in trouble the minute I picked him up from school by picking on one of his sisters or talking back to me. I would stop the car and ask, "Christian, would you say that to Mrs. Emly?"

"No, Mama," he would reply sheepishly.

"You need to show me even more respect than you show your teacher," I would say. I actually felt a little jealous that he cared more about earning her approval than attaining mine.

One morning Christian asked my husband, David, if he could take a dead snake to school, which we had killed in our yard two days earlier. "The kids will love it for show-and-tell," he pleaded.

"Sure, you can take it," his dad replied. I cringed as they trotted off into the woods to put the dead snake into a jar.

When they returned, I stared into the jar and examined the snake from every angle. There are a few words which are not proper to say in my southern family. Suffice it to say, I was inspecting the snake for "fly larva." Finding no positive indicators, I warned my son, "Do not take this jar out of the paper sack until you have permission from Mrs. Emly." Suddenly I was the one concerned with what his teacher might think.

As I walked toward his classroom after school, one of the boys from his room hugged me and proclaimed, "Oh, Mrs. Humbert, thank you for letting Christian bring the snake to school today! It was *way cool*!" I smiled to myself, glad I had not made a mistake by allowing Christian to display his "trophy" to the class.

As I neared the room, Christian and several of the boys were jumping up and down with delight. "Look, Mama, look!" Christian squealed. "I showed the snake at lunch, but we just pulled the jar out of the bag, and the snake and the inside of the jar are covered with maggots!"

My face flushed red. I wanted to hide from embarrassment! My son had said the word *maggots* in front of his teacher! I had only seen maggots once, and I knew those horrid creatures were enough to turn even a cast-iron stomach sour. Before I was halfway through my apology, Mrs. Emly was laughing. "It's no big deal," she said with a grin. "It was a wonderful science lesson. The kids were thrilled to see the snake, but they were even more excited to see the appearance of the maggots! His show-and-tell presentation was like two for the price of one!

"I did learn something important," she continued. "Christian says he is bringing a tarantula tomorrow. From now on, when he brings a critter, I plan to move show-and-tell to the afternoon instead of during lunchtime."

"That sounds like a wise idea," I agreed.

That day, I learned an important lesson from a sweet, laid-back, young teacher. Children thrive and learn more easily when the person teaching them is relaxed about the realities of nature and real life. I realized that I was uptight over anything that didn't look or sound "ladylike." But the beautiful Mrs. Emly taught me to laugh and find the teaching opportunity even in the grossest creatures my children drag out of the woods.

* * *

Let my teaching fall like rain and my words descend like dew, like showers on new grass, like abundant rain on tender plants.

Deuteronomy 32:2

class clown

Vicki Caruana

....

Humour is mankind's greatest blessing.

Mark Twain

When I was in school, I was the kind of student every teacher wanted — I was compliant, quiet, and I completed my assignments. When I was in high school, I remember getting annoyed with those who caused problems in the classroom. Kids who passed notes, whispered behind the teacher's back, and raised their hand just to get a laugh were getting in the way of my learning! I believed that the class clown had a lot to learn, and I wished he (it was usually a *he*) would just cut it out and get to work.

When I became a teacher, I was still compliant, quiet, and industrious. I wanted to be every principal's dream. I sought out and took as much of the advice veteran teachers were willing to offer. *Never smile before Christmas. Don't laugh at their jokes. Maintain classroom discipline above all else.* These words seemed logical to me. After all, I was their teacher, not their friend. I was in control and they shouldn't be.

And then there was Justin.

Justin was my first class clown. Not a day went by that he didn't interrupt some lesson with his quick wit. He saw "funny" written all over everything. I knew I had to be careful with a class clown. He could easily take over my class, and I decided early on that this would never happen in my class.

But it became a challenge to Justin to make me laugh. Justin realized that I wasn't an easy target and whatever he did had to be planned carefully. He completed all of his work so I wouldn't have anything to complain about. What Justin didn't know was that I was struggling every day *not* to laugh. I didn't want to give him the satisfaction.

It was getting harder and harder for me to maintain my composure. Justin was hilarious! The more I avoided making eye contact, the more Justin attracted attention to himself. I started to get really stressed about the whole thing, feeling like a failure of a teacher for being tempted to laugh at the class clown. I began getting tension headaches and ended each day in a grumpy mood.

Keep in mind, Justin's humor wasn't crude or rude. In fact, he had a talent for making people laugh. His impersonations alone could bring the house down. Then one day it happened. I let go and laughed out loud! The class was shocked — the clown was jubilant! I was incredibly relieved. My headaches stopped, and I realized that laughter really was the best medicine. I indulged in a dose every day from then on.

A disciplined classroom is one thing, but a tension-filled one is quite another. Children don't learn well under stress. If handled well, laughter can be used to your advantage. Justin taught me more about creating an effective learning environment than any of the veteran teachers whose advice I initially sought.

So let your students see you laugh and let them glimpse your heart. I know we give God plenty of reasons to laugh. My carefully laid-out plan for a disciplined classroom must have made him roll over laughing.

. . . .

A cheerful heart is good medicine,
but a crushed spirit dries up the bones.

PROVERBS 17:22

grocery store encouragement

Kim Stafford-Galaviz

· ·

If I were two-faced, would I be wearing this one?

Abraham Lincoln

Some time ago I took my two youngest daughters, ages five and three, to the grocery store. It was going to be a quick trip. All we needed was some hamburger and a gallon of milk. I was in a pair of scummy jeans and my face was void of makeup. I didn't have time to devote to my appearance that afternoon. Just keeping up with my young daughters was like watching fan blades spinning at full speed.

As a full-time middle school teacher and a mother of three girls, my days and nights were filled with constant lively chatter and nonstop discipline issues. I was having "one of those days," when little bothersome things mount up until there's an avalanche. While my life was fun, my schedule was exhausting.

In the evenings it seemed the laundry piled up right along with the garbage. I literally fell into bed each night.

At the grocery store that day, my older daughter, Olivia, ran off. Abby, my toddler, began yelling about wanting candy. I was once again given the opportunity to choose patience. That's when I passed a young woman in the cereal aisle. She looked vaguely familiar, but she didn't seem to recognize me, so I just kept searching for Olivia.

Five minutes later, with both girls in tow, I headed for the dairy section. I felt a tap on my shoulder. I turned around, and there was the "Cereal Aisle Girl." She smiled at me with a look of recognition. I thought, *I really should have put my makeup on today*.

"Is your name Miss Stafford?" (Stafford was my maiden name.)

"Oh, Krissy! I thought I knew you!" Krissy had been one of my students nine years earlier. She used to call my then-fiancé "Mr. Stafford," which irritated him more than a little during our courtship and engagement period.

We chatted while my girls stared at her. She had long blonde hair, a beautiful complexion, and an air of confidence. She had really come a long way since those awkward middle school years! I introduced my two girls and told her what I'd been doing since her graduation from the eighth grade. Krissy shared her upcoming plans for college, which included a trip to Zurich, Switzerland, to study German.

"Wow!" I said. "That's awesome!"

"It's because of *you*," she glowed.

I felt my eyebrows go up.

"It is," she insisted. "You taught me French at the Christian school, and that's how I became interested in foreign languages. You had a huge impact on my life!"

At that moment everything came to a stop. All the stresses of the day melted away — the dirty dishes, the ungraded essays, my lack of makeup, my frumpy outfit, and my frustration with overactive children. God was giving me one lesson in priorities and another in grace. He had sent a gentle reminder of his faithfulness and love, which are so much greater than all the little things that were causing my anxiety. I left the grocery store that day feeling encouraged and significant.

"Mommy, who was that?" Olivia asked as we got into the car.

"One of my former students," I replied. Suddenly my role as a teacher felt like a high and holy calling. "C'mon, kids, let's go home."

* * *

He lifted me out of the slimy pit, out of the mud and mire;
he set my feet on a rock and gave me a firm place to stand.

PSALM 40:2

55

the teacher's uniform

Vicki Caruana

· ·

*My business is not to remake myself, but [to] make the
absolute best of what God made.*

ROBERT BROWNING

My first day teaching in a middle school was
quite an eye-opener. Look at that! His pants
looked like a Scottish kilt. Look at the jewelry
store displayed on that gal. My goodness, look at all the propa-
ganda buttons pinned to those two. You can tell they are best
friends — they dress exactly alike. And how about the guy who
showed up on a motorcycle wearing leather *everything*.

And look at the hair on some of these people. I wished
mine was long enough to wear in a ponytail like that guy's. I
realized people have been dyeing their hair odd colors, but
blue — puh-lease! Look at that gal in the library. Her dread-
locks matched the native dress she wore. And I thought students dressed oddly. Who knew that teachers didn't follow a
dress code either?

56

I must have seemed awfully conservative compared to everyone else. I wore dress pants and a stylish blouse with no jewelry, and since my hair is red to begin with, I wore it au naturel.

Although I dressed conservatively, one of my goals as a teacher was never to look like a teacher. My image of teachers was that they tended to dress either out of style or wear a denim jumper covered with "I love teaching" pins. My goal? Style and comfort. No high heels because I was on my feet all day, and stylish enough not to be snickered at by the students behind my back.

I thought I had accomplished my goal until one day early in the school year.

"You're late, young lady!" an irritated matronly voice boomed from behind me.

The bell had already rung, and I was the only one in the hallway — I thought.

"No, you don't understand," I said, already feeling like a child caught in wrongdoing. "I'm on my break. I don't have a class this period."

"You look just like one of the students, dear," she said, without apology. "Consider dressing more like a teacher tomorrow."

I was mortified. I'm what you would call a "good girl" and do what I am told. I hated being treated like a "girl" instead of a professional.

The next day I dressed a little more formally. A jacket accompanied my stylish dress pants and blouse, and I wore pearls. Thank goodness I love pearls. Oh, and one more thing — a pin that said, "Did you read a book today?" It was just enough to appease the powers-that-be without making me the subject of whispered ridicule. That day the forced smile from the blue-haired lady was all the affirmation I needed.

I can't control what other teachers wear to school. But I can make sure that what I wear doesn't distract either teachers or students from who I am — a good teacher.

* * *

I also want women to dress modestly, with decency and propriety, not with braided hair or gold or pearls or expensive clothes, but with good deeds, appropriate for women who profess to worship God.

1 TIMOTHY 2:9 – 10

endings and beginnings

Bernadine Johnson

· ·

Da capo al fine

ITALIAN: GO BACK TO THE BEGINNING AND PLAY TO THE END

I'm a piano teacher, which is really amazing when you take into account that I made up an entire new middle section to Beethoven's *Moonlight Sonata* during my eighth grade concert.

What I love about teaching piano is that often a student begins in kindergarten and studies piano until leaving for college. That adds up to a lot of hours around a piano together — sharing music, talking about life, laughing, and crying. I am always the teacher, but sometime during those years I also become a mother, a counselor, and a friend.

Allison was a dream student. She was one who evoked words like *incredible*.

Her giftedness made me look good!

Allison and I filled the pages of our history together with her first car, her first automobile accident, her first guitar, her first concerto, and her parents' divorce. Allison and I grew up together, and in some ways, we taught each other. She didn't know how to read music. I didn't know how to read people. We both learned what we needed to learn and fell in love with each other in the process.

It was the end of August when she came to her final lesson. She was going to college the next week and would be studying piano with someone else. I was feeling some anxiety, knowing I was turning her out into the world with *my* imprint. Had I told her all the important things? Had she listened?

As our last lesson came to a close, I knew it was time to cut the cord. I walked outside with my student into the sun, hoping the warmth would soothe the pain. We stood on the porch of my studio, both gulping, both dreading the end. It was Allison who spoke first, "Let's not say 'good-bye.' Let's just say, 'See ya downtown.'"

We live in a small Michigan town where most people know each other. I've had mail addressed to me with just my name and the zip code, and the post office always knows where to deliver it. In fact, it's the kind of town where the lady at Radio Shack will let you know if your son tried to rent a bad movie. (I know this from personal experience.) So, when Allison suggested we'd see each other downtown, I thought it was a way of hanging on to one of the apron strings.

As I hugged Allison on the porch, a car pulled into the driveway. It was my next student, Meagan, age seven, arriving for her first lesson. She was dressed in a party dress. Black patent leather shoes completed her outfit. Brown curls flowed to her waist. As a mother of three boys, I drooled. I asked her if she was going to a party after her lesson, to which she replied, "No, I dressed up for *you*." (Gulp.)

Each new student is like a clean sheet of manuscript paper. Some will turn out with simple melodies; some are more elaborate. When one song is completed, there is always another one to start. God continually allows me a new beginning and puts his trust in me to love the teaching process and to love the child. I am amazed and humbled.

Allison held up her hand in a final wave as I guided Meagan in to begin her first lesson.

. . . .

There's an opportune time to do things, a right time for everything on the earth: A right time to cry and another to laugh, A right time to lament and another to cheer, . . .
A right time to embrace and another to part, . . .
A right time to hold on and another to let go.

Ecclesiastes 3:1, 4–6 MSG

order in the classroom!

Vicki Caruana

. . . .

I must create a system, or be enslaved by another man's.

WILLIAM BLAKE

*T*eachers' classrooms have a tendency to fall into chaos once the school year gets going. Even the most organized of us struggle to keep our hands on all the paperwork that we and our students generate each and every day. I learned early on that maintaining order in my classroom had more to do with orderliness than student discipline.

Besides being a classroom teacher, I hosted the staffing meeting (meeting to discuss and place exceptional education students) each week in my room. I was responsible for making sure that the meeting was announced and attendance was confirmed. I also attended a faculty meeting, a department meeting, or a district meeting every week. Tons of paperwork accompanied each one of those get-togethers. I also sponsored a student drama club and tutored struggling students after school. Paperwork, paperwork, and more paperwork!

Then there were the five classes I taught and all of their homework to grade, data to input into the computer, progress reports to write and distribute and make three copies of. I had to contact every parent at least once and document either the phone call or the conference — in triplicate — and file the appropriate copies in the front office and the district office. The mail that showed up in my teacher mailbox every day almost always required me to take some sort of action. I had to document that as well.

We were always told that in order to cover ourselves, we needed to document, document, document. And we did.

It's so easy to let things slide. In the beginning of each year I started out making sure that I didn't leave the building until my desk was cleared and anything that required my attention was attended to. By the beginning of February it was hard to remember why that was important — until my son was in kindergarten.

When my oldest child started school, he attended where I taught. I thought it would make life easier. It did in many ways. I always knew where he was and could look in on him whenever I wanted. I was thrilled that he got the teacher I requested. My son needed someone who would loosen him up a little and help him learn how to have fun while he learned. From other parent accounts, this was the teacher he needed. Her creative reputation was well known. In spite of her good reputation, however, I should have taken a warning from the fact that on the first day, this teacher's classroom was already in chaos. I just thought she was "creative." She was that, but she was also quite absentminded and readily admitted that to both her students and their parents. As long as her abstract-random personality didn't adversely affect my son, it didn't bother me.

But she lost his report card. She couldn't find the homework he turned in. She wasn't quite prepared for Open House, and his work wasn't displayed. And she forgot about the conference we set up twice! Any confidence I had in this teacher dissipated by November.

The good thing that came out of her chaos was that I became painfully aware of the importance of being organized. Staying organized is no easy task. Things just want to fall apart. I purposefully made sure that all my paperwork was filed, my calendar was up-to-date, and that I kept my word to both students and parents. My reputation was at stake and I wanted to do everything I could not to disappoint a student or parent the way we were disappointed.

When you are operating without order, it's God's reputation that is on the line. When others see you, they see him. Our God is a God of order and purpose. He does nothing haphazardly or without a plan. We can aspire to be just like him and follow in the path he has set before us. Then blessings — and not disappointments — are sure to follow!

. . . .

But everything should be done in a fitting and orderly way.

1 CORINTHIANS 14:40

junior high hormones

Carol Kent

. . . .

> *I was a fantastic student until ten,*
> *and then my mind began to wander.*
>
> **GRACE PALEY**

*a*t the age of twenty-three I accepted the position of teaching English, drama, and speech at Fremont Junior High. I was motivated to make a difference in the lives of my students. I looked forward to the challenge of motivating and inspiring young teens to love great literature and to discover the joy of public speaking.

I was assigned the advanced track of seventh and eighth grade English students, and I eagerly anticipated the opportunity to challenge above-average minds. With careful penmanship, I wrote a quotation across the chalkboard to stimulate the brains of my new charges. It was from Will Rogers: "We are all ignorant; we are just ignorant about different things." The eighth graders took their places in my first-hour class. They appeared to be well behaved and interested in learning.

Ten minutes later I discovered Mike. He fidgeted, tapped his pencil incessantly on the desk, blew spit balls through a straw when he thought I wasn't watching, talked out loud to the students next to him — and didn't quit when I gave him my direct eye contact "I-can-beat-you-at-this-game" teacher look. In fact, he enjoyed staring back at me with a grimace on his face that seemed to defy all authority. I hesitated to send him to the principal's office because it would make me — a new teacher — look like I was incapable of controlling my students. *Had Mike already sensed my reluctance to discipline him due to my own fear of failure?*

While I was still looking in his direction, Mike read aloud part of the quotation on the board: "Hey, teacher — good quote! 'We are all ignorant.'" He stopped without reading the rest of Will Rogers' meaningful statement. "So how are *you* ignorant, Mrs. Kent?" he asked with a sneer.

I quickly realized the respect I would get (or not get) from the entire class might hinge on this first verbal confrontation with my hormone-driven junior high student, whom I now assume had ADD (Attention Deficit Disorder) long before the disorder had been labeled.

Pausing only briefly, I responded, "Thanks for asking, Mike. A lot of students might think that's an inappropriate question, but on your first try, you came up with the whole point of today's lesson. Congratulations!"

Mike's body language relaxed and his eyebrows arched as he took on a facial expression of surprise and pride in his accomplishment. "Er . . . ah . . . well . . . thanks," he mumbled under his breath.

I explained, this time to the whole class, "We're going to discuss how each of us is an expert on a unique topic because we come from so many different backgrounds and experiences. We *are* ignorant about some things — but only because we haven't taken the time to get informed. I'd like to spend time getting to know each of you personally this school year, and I hope you'll make the time to get to know each other. Your final assignment, at the end of the first semester, will be to give a five-minute speech on a topic you are an expert on that will help to educate all of us in your area of expertise."

Glancing down the row at my challenging student, I continued, "Mike, since you commented on the Will Rogers quotation first, I'd like to start by meeting with you for a few minutes after class today. We can brainstorm about some speech topics you might be interested in presenting." To my surprise, he nodded in agreement.

That day Mike became my friend as well as my student. He still had occasional bouts of thirteen-year-old hormonal responses, but there was an underlying respect and a foundation upon which we built a healthy student-teacher relationship. The school year ended on a positive note.

Three years passed. An unexpected visitor stuck his head in my classroom after school. The face looked vaguely familiar. "Hey, Mrs. Kent. Remember me? Mike? Your perpetual challenge in eighth grade English?"

Rising from my seat, I smiled, greeted him warmly, and invited him in. "I just wanted to tell you how much I appreciated your class," he told me. "On my first day in here, when I was trying my best to be a troublemaker, you made me think about what I'm best at — electronics. That quote: 'We are all ignorant; we are just ignorant about different things,' got me to thinking about how much I love taking radios and TVs apart. I've discovered I'm really good at that and I thought you — of all people — should know I'm going to college in another year. I'm planning to major in electrical engineering. Thanks for putting up with me and for seeing my potential in spite of my weird antics."

That day I remembered why I chose teaching as my profession. I planted seeds in the minds of my students that later took root and flourished. In my four years as a junior high teacher, I grew to understand and love my complex, highly creative, emotionally irrepressible, hormonally charged seventh and eighth graders. I threw my heart and soul into a profession that allowed me to succeed at what I did best — teach!

Whatever your hand finds to do, do it with all your might.

ECCLESIASTES 9:10

sticky fingers and
sticky floors

Vicki Caruana

· ·

Charity is no substitute for justice withheld.

SAINT AUGUSTINE

*M*y new black heels stubbornly stuck to the cafeteria floor. Why did I wear these today? I certainly knew better. I was afraid to even look down and find out what mysterious adhesive was hindering my progress during lunch duty. It was just the beginning of my thirty-minute vigil, and I eyed the clock on the wall only to discover I still had twenty-eight minutes left!

I was on the hunt during lunch duty. Any impropriety on the part of students would be caught and dealt with. I had my whistle. I had my walkie-talkie (on loan to me from the assistant principal), a tool denoting status and power. I had my referral slips tightly clutched in my hand just waiting to be filled out. Unfortunately, I was still stuck to the floor! And now students around me were beginning to notice.

That's when I saw it — a spoon filled with an unidentifiable substance (could have been mashed potatoes, could have been Elmer's glue) poised to be released toward a group of unsuspecting eighth grade girls at the next table. The sharpshooter hadn't yet noticed that I had noticed his foul intent. Normally this would be a simple matter to curb, but the impending food fight was three tables away from me. My only hope was to sprint from my current position, leap across two of the tables, and catch the flung spoon in midair. What I wouldn't have given to be a stunt woman from *Crouching Tiger, Hidden Dragon*! I settled for a hurried walk.

With my first step I stepped right out of my new black pumps and stood in my stocking feet on the still sticky floor. Ugh! What in the world was on this floor? I looked down to discover a spilled can of soda all over the path in front of me. Parts of the floor were still wet, so instead of sticking, I slid. I slid right past two tables of snickering teenagers and into the boy with the spoon.

He never saw it coming.

I fell into him and we both fell onto the sickeningly slippery floor. Gotcha! By this time a crowd had gathered, and the would-be victims of a pudding attack (I found out later it was tapioca pudding on that spoon) pulled me to my feet. I yanked the spoon from the bewildered seventh grade boy's hand and sat down to write out his discipline referral. I then led him out of the cafeteria, grabbing my stray shoes on our way out.

I've never liked lunch duty. It is the loudest, most out-of-control thirty minutes any teacher could ever spend. But somehow, on that particular day, I gained the reputation of the all-knowing, all-seeing, and all-terrain teacher. Kids were on their toes when I was on duty.

It's hard not to tire in doing what is right. Sometimes we're discouraged. Sometimes we're tired. And sometimes — not often — we're humiliated. Walking a student to the office in sticky stockings was definitely not a proud moment. God calls us to do what is right, even if it means making a fool of ourselves. I don't mind being a fool for God.

Let us not become weary in doing good, for at the proper time we will reap a harvest if we do not give up.

GALATIANS 6:9

the little pink bookmark

Judith Conger

I have the power to mold, to nurture, to hold, to hug, to love, to cajole, to praise . . . to point out pathways . . . to become part of another person's well-being. What could be more powerful?

MARVA COLLINS

*D*uring my early years of teaching first grade in the sixties, I employed the accepted method of reading instruction. Like a mother hen with her bevy of chicks, I would sit with a group of my six-year-old charges perched on small chairs arranged in a semicircle in front of me. I would then reveal the secrets of the written word as we delved through our volumes of *Dick and Jane.*

Step One: *Motivate.* "Robins (the name the students had bestowed upon their small reading group), look at Jane pulling Sally in the little red wagon. Why do you think Jane is giving her a ride?" I would refer to the pictures in the book to motivate my students to read the printed page. After two or three responses were offered, I would move on.

Step Two: *Read Silently*. I gave my students their next instructions: "Read the page and see what you think." Since it doesn't take much time to read "Come, Sally. Come. Come," we moved on quickly.

Step Three: *Read Orally*. I began this step with a query: "Who would like to read the page aloud?" Two or three students would proudly demonstrate their skills.

Step Four: *Draw Conclusions*. I threw out the question, "Where do you think Jane is taking Sally? Do you think little Sally wants to go? Let's turn the page and find out."

Motivate, read silently, read orally, draw conclusions.

Apparently my well-prepared and carefully executed teaching method was not motivating little Caleb. The denim jeans he wore to school that day had a hole in the crotch. During the silent reading step, he reached through the opening in his jeans, beyond his briefs, and pulled out his male plumbing. Without a word, Caleb placed his "little pink bookmark" in the spine of the opened book on his lap!

My bachelor of science degree in education had not prepared me for this moment. I didn't want to draw attention to his performance and embarrass him in front of the rest of the reading group. I also didn't want to startle him, which could cause serious injury if he chose to close the book quickly. I waited for what seemed like a never-ending minute. Finally we made eye contact. I looked down at the "bookmark" and then into his eyes. Slowly I shook my head back and forth, indicating my disapproval of his action.

Caleb immediately picked up on my nonverbal communication. He nonchalantly tucked his "equipment" back into the same hole it had come out of, and we continued the lesson with no one else in the class aware of what had transpired.

That day Caleb taught me an important lesson. The "nonverbal" part of my teaching career is just as important as the spoken word. My attitude, demeanor, eye contact, and body language often speak louder than words.

* * *

Therefore, as God's chosen people, holy and dearly loved, clothe yourselves with compassion, kindness, humility, gentleness and patience.

Colossians 3:12

teacher divas

Vicki Caruana

. . . .

No act of kindness, no matter how small, is ever wasted.

AESOP

*D*uring my first faculty meeting at a new school, I couldn't help but notice I was now in a more prosperous district. Not only was I pleasantly surprised to find an increased teacher budget but it also seemed as if the income level of some of the teachers was quite elevated compared to that of my previous district. As my mother would say, they were "dressed to the nines." They were dripping in jewelry. They drove BMWs and Mercedes! I felt like Dorothy stepping out of her run-down, tornado-ridden house and into the colorful collage of Oz.

And I seriously wondered if I belonged.

You see, for some reason I have often ended up as the poor girl living in a rich neighborhood. When I became a teacher I sort of thought we all were like nuns or monks — we took a vow of poverty. It was expected. Money was never a motivator to become or remain a teacher. But now, at a time when I made more as a teacher than my husband did and buying groceries often felt like a luxury, I was again surrounded by the rich.

Do I sound bitter? I wasn't bitter, I was flabbergasted!

I wondered how they could be making so much more money than I did. Had they been teaching that much longer? They didn't seem old enough for that. Some didn't have children yet. They were DINKS (Double-Income, No Kids), but so were we. I found out that their husbands made more money than God (and I know—I've seen our church's monthly offering)! These women didn't even *need* to work. Then it occurred to me: maybe they were teaching because they wanted to change lives, because they loved kids. Just like me! Maybe we had more in common than I thought.

I thought wrong. I discovered early on that what drove these women into the classroom was the paycheck, the time off in the summer, and time out of the house.

All this became painfully obvious as I tried in vain to form friendships with my new colleagues. They had formed a tight clique that was not accepting new members. It felt like high school all over again! I didn't dress the way they did. I didn't hang out with the same people they did. I didn't complain about the principal behind her back like they did. And then I made a fatal error—I parked in one of *their* spaces. Never mind that these weren't official parking spaces. Never mind that no one warned me about the secret parking rules. The wrath of the

Divas was upon me! I was blacklisted, and it felt as if they were putting stumbling blocks in my way at every turn.

At the beginning of the next year I wanted to help sponsor the yearbook committee. I had previous experience and loved it — but two of the Divas were already part of that committee and made it clear they didn't *need* me. The same thing happened with the school newspaper, the drama club, and the Future Teachers of America club. I felt shut out — ostracized.

I started to sequester myself in my classroom during lunch, during my planning periods, before and after school. I remembered learning about pain avoidance in behavior modification class in college. I knew that's what I was doing, but I wasn't willing to put myself into a painful situation if I didn't need to. By midyear I started to consider putting in for a voluntary transfer for the next year. I didn't think I could handle this much longer.

Then one of the top Divas had emergency surgery, which left a gaping hole in the drama club. The performance was only weeks away and someone needed to step in and take over. I felt the shove of the Holy Spirit and volunteered. The principal was grateful, but the other Divas looked at me like a pride of lionesses daring a new female to set foot into their territory.

The production was a rousing success, and the Diva I replaced made it to the performance. When the students handed me a dozen roses in appreciation, I left the spotlight to hand them to Sherry (yes, the Diva had a name). I led the audience in a standing ovation for her because it was her hard work that really prepared those kids.

Slowly, ever so slowly, things began to change (at least the overt acts of hostility stopped). I wasn't sure if I had made a friend or crushed an enemy. At the very least, it was the start of a peaceful coexistence.

Even if a person comes to teaching out of impure motives, we need to treat her with dignity and respect.

* * *

On the contrary: "If your enemy is hungry, feed him; if he is thirsty, give him something to drink. In doing this, you will heap burning coals on his head." Do not be overcome by evil, but overcome evil with good.

ROMANS 12:20–21

pet picture day

Janet Fleck

. . . .

*A well-developed sense of humor is the pole that adds balance to
your steps as you walk the tightrope of life.*

WILLIAM A. WARD

*J*t was barely 9:00 a.m., but everyone's nerves were
already frazzled. What was supposed to be a fun,
orderly, calm fund-raiser was turning into my worst
nightmare. Every teacher and principal can probably think of
a school event that began like a disaster and ended as a fond,
humorous memory — but only after enough time passes to erase
the pain. Pet Picture Day at Kreeger Elementary School was
that kind of an experience.

The salesman had promised, "All you have to do is send out
the promotional flyers and provide the room for us to set up our
photography equipment. We'll do all the work." I believed him.
After all, he was the expert. His company had sponsored many
such events. Besides, I knew what picture days were like because

the children had their school pictures taken once a year. One classroom at a time would be dismissed and the teachers would quickly and in an orderly manner line up the children. They would walk to the designated room, get their pictures taken, and return to their classroom. The entire process took only a few hours.

As principal of a well-respected elementary school, I envisioned this same orderly procedure on Pet Picture Day, so I trusted the salesman's judgment about not scheduling parents to bring their children's pets to school at specific, staggered times. "Oh, no, Mrs. Fleck," he insisted, "appointments are not necessary." He promised that everything would be fine if the parents brought their children's pets whenever they wanted to during the two hours reserved for photos: 9:00 a.m. to 11:00 a.m.

It quickly became apparent that I had greatly underestimated the popularity of Pet Picture Day. The "come when you want to come" plan had flaws, and the teachers in my building were *not* happy as the drama surrounding this event unfolded.

To my dismay, approximately two hundred parents chose to arrive at 9:00 a.m. sharp, hoping to be first in line. The parking lot was in chaos because it could not hold all the cars. The diversity of pets being unloaded from vehicles surprised me. I had expected cats, dogs, a guinea pig or two, and perhaps some hamsters. I did not expect goats, lambs, rabbits, snakes, iguanas and other lizards — and I certainly did not expect to see one parent struggling to unload three llamas.

Getting the animals out of the vehicles was easy. Getting them into the building and down the hallway to the room designated as the photography studio was nearly impossible. The huge llamas, cousins to the camel, *did not*, thank goodness, spit foul-smelling saliva in our faces as they are likely to do when irritated. However, they stubbornly refused to enter the building.

The lambs, goats, and large dogs were on leashes. Unable to get traction on the well-waxed floor, they slipped and slid their way down the hall, whining all the way.

I had not anticipated how all those frightened pets would respond when they and their owners were crowded into lines on both sides of a school hallway too small for all the commotion. High-pitched squeals of excited children blended with their pets' barks, howls, growls, whines, baas, hisses, and meows ricocheting off the tile walls.

Small animals leaped out of parents' arms. Large dogs strained against leashes, snarled and sniffed at each other, and marked their turfs. Puddles appeared all over the floor. When I asked the janitor to please get a mop and clean up the mess, he said, "This isn't what I was hired for." So I dragged the mop out of the janitor's closet and fought a losing battle the rest of the morning.

Eventually, all the pictures got taken and the puddles were mopped up, but the teachers in my building were quick to let me know that Pet Picture Day was *not* the picture-perfect day I had envisioned. By the end of the day, the teachers were barely speaking to me.

Several weeks later, their irritation subsided when they learned that Pet Picture Day had generated several thousand dollars for the school — dollars earmarked for summer teacher in-service education.

For the record, that was Kreeger Elementary School's *first* and *last* Pet Picture Day. Now the teachers smile as they recall the faces of excited, happy children proudly posing for pictures with their beloved pets. All of us agreed there was much to be thankful for: Pet Picture Day was successful — and we will be laughing out loud for years to come as we recall a day none of us hopes to live through again!

* * *

Be cheerful no matter what; pray all the time; thank God no matter what happens. This is the way God wants you who belong to Christ Jesus to live.

1 THESSALONIANS 5:16 – 18 MSG

and baby makes 33!

Vicki Caruana

. . . .

Two roads diverged into a wood,
and I — I took the one less traveled by,

And that has made all the difference.

ROBERT FROST

School buildings become our second homes, and if we're lucky, our colleagues become our second family. I had taught at my school for only three years when I left to have my first child. I was just getting to the point where I felt like I belonged. It was a large middle school with 1,400 students and more than a hundred teachers. I knew so few of them. There is precious little time to form lasting relationships with colleagues. My classes all had about thirty-two students in them.

Saying good-bye is never easy for me — especially with students. They become my own children during the year we are together. I always ended a year with mixed emotions — proud they were moving on and desperate not to let them go.

I had taken a lot of grief from some of my colleagues about my decision to stay at home with my baby and not come back to work. The criticism made me feel a little less sad about leaving. But my students and their parents treated me with care and loving concern. They would miss me, but they were excited for me as well. They watched as my belly expanded and came to refer to this baby as *their* baby as well. It was no surprise to me when, a few days before I was to leave that school forever, the parents gave me a baby shower.

And I was tempted — for a little while — to seriously consider coming back to work after six weeks. I felt confident as a teacher. I knew what I was doing. I knew how to train young minds, mold behavior, and touch the hearts of my students. For some reason, I questioned whether I could really do the same for my own flesh and blood. There was no teacher's manual for this subject. No in-service training. No supervised practice. I would be alone in this assignment. As a teacher, at least I'd spend part of my day doing something I knew I could do well.

That temptation didn't last long. To my utter surprise, the faculty threw me a baby shower attended by even the male teachers. Colleagues who once were so discouraging appeared envious of my choice to stay home. The veteran teachers, the ones who had already raised their own children, applauded me. It was as if they were commissioning me to go out on an incredible journey. As the head custodian walked me out to my car with the last of my classroom supplies, he hugged me and said,

"We're sure going to miss you around here." He paused and I thought I saw a stray tear escape from his weathered laugh lines. "This son of yours is a lucky fellow. He gets to be with you all day, every day."

Today, twelve years later as the parent of a middle school child, I can walk into any school and feel as if I belong there. That's a gift. Most parents feel awkward and out of place when they enter a school building. Some even feel anxious and uncomfortable as they relive their own school experiences. But to me a school is a place of love and acceptance, of shared experiences and common challenges. I guess what they say is true — you can take the teacher out of school, but you can't take the school out of the teacher. That, indeed, is a good feeling.

· ·

*Do not repay evil with evil or insult with insult,
but with blessing, because to this you were called so that
you may inherit a blessing.*

1 PETER 3:9

the taj mahal

Vicki Caruana

. . . .

We have met the enemy, and he is us.

WALT KELLY

*F*inding ways to balance teaching and motherhood is never easy. I left the classroom when I had our first child, but I stayed "connected" in a variety of ways. One year I was hired by the district to write curriculum from home. The only catch was that I had to be on site one full day per week. Thank goodness my mother was willing to baby-sit. I thought it was the perfect job for that season in my life. What I didn't expect was a change in attitude.

Part of my responsibility was to attend meetings on behalf of our department at the district's administration building, christened the Taj Mahal by teachers who were convinced the lavish building was a result of many years of minuscule pay increases. Anyone who worked in the Taj Mahal was branded as "the enemy." Now I worked there.

The odd thing I discovered was that the people who worked in this palatial place didn't have long fangs and clawlike appendages with the remains of downtrodden teachers they had devoured hanging from them. Nor did they act like the KGB, watching our every move, waiting for us to come out into the light so they could shoot us down. The supervisors and administrators I came to know were genuinely concerned about both the teachers and the students. They agonized over the budgets. They hated the paperwork they were inundated with. They cursed the days when all they seemed to do was attend meeting after meeting without accomplishing anything. The expressionless faces of those at the threshold of burnout were the same faces I saw on teachers.

For the first time I understood what it was like to *lead* in the school system. It wasn't rewarding in the same way that teachers get rewards. Administrators didn't get thank-yous or Christmas presents or the thrill of watching a student they had struggled with graduate with honors. Their rewards were few and far apart. They also had to deal with accusatory words from the same teachers they worked so hard to protect. Have you ever felt as if you couldn't do anything right? Would you like to feel that on a regular basis? Become an administrator.

I couldn't keep this revelation to myself. I took every opportunity to talk about working in the Taj Mahal and what it was really like. Few teachers wanted to listen. Instead they turned on me, accusing me of sleeping with the enemy or being brainwashed.

My assignment at the Taj Mahal was short-lived, not because I couldn't stand the heat but because it began to demand too much of my time. When I left, I felt like I was abandoning people who desperately needed to be encouraged. The forlorn look in their eyes reminded me of a shipwrecked crew left on a desert island.

Ideally, all teachers should "serve time" in their respective Taj Mahals. I learned there is no *us* and *them* — just us. We are all in this business of teaching together, for the sake of the children. We all need encouragement and appreciation. And those are things we can give to one another. Use the gift of encouragement that God has given you. When we encourage one another, we can all win!

And what does the Lord require of you? To act justly and to love mercy and to walk humbly with your God.

MICAH 6:8

the river city good time band

Carole Brewer

When you follow your bliss . . . doors will open where you would not have thought there would be doors; and where there wouldn't be a door for anyone else.

JOSEPH CAMPBELL

*W*hen my husband Jan, a professional drummer, and I, a trained singer and pianist, arrived on the special education scene in the late seventies, the expectations for the mentally challenged to perform were incredibly low. If individuals could bang out a tune on an instrument or sing a song — any song — most parents and teachers were satisfied. Music was most often incorporated into special education programs only for its therapeutic value.

Unaware of existing articles and textbook theories on the subject of teaching music to mentally challenged students, we volunteered to start a music class at a summer camp.

Our proposal was approved by the Association for Retarded Citizens, whose activity director recruited the loudest and hammiest performers at camp. The students came because it was a chance to get out of their "board and care homes" for the evening and enjoy what they thought was a really cool "jam session."

Within a few weeks, we made our second proposal: "We will continue as the teachers for this music class with the understanding that the participants will prepare a program and enter an upcoming performing arts competition."

The students said, "Okay!" not realizing the challenging six months of hard work ahead of them, and the parents agreed to continue with their support.

During that hot Sacramento summer, in a classroom with no air conditioning and a pathetic piano, we all pressed forward, putting together a half-hour program of pop, gospel, and patriotic songs. Besides the musical training, we gave lessons in stage presence, social graces, and grooming. "Smile!" and "Let's try again!" came out of my mouth hundreds of times. I labeled our teaching style "creative repetition."

Our extraordinary adult students were Joe, who played my husband's drum set; Nick, a self-taught guitarist; multi-talented Ross, who played violin and viola accompaniments on a synthesizer; and our on-pitch enthusiastic singers — Charla, Laura, Dennis, and Ken. My husband taught himself to play the bass guitar, and my piano skills improved considerably.

The anticipated October day arrived, and it was our group's turn to perform before the audience and judges. Those long hours of rehearsal really paid off, because the songs went like clockwork. After each musical selection the audience, amazed with the quality of the presentation, gave a huge round of applause. At the start of the last song, Joe accidentally hit his knee on the bottom of the snare drum. It flipped off its stand and rolled toward the center aisle. Dutifully, the rest of us followed our motto: "Keep going no matter what!" while Joe got up from his stool to chase the runaway drum. Catching it right in front of the judges, he quickly carried it back, repositioned it on its stand, sat down, and grabbed a stick just in time to hit the last beat of the song. We won the competition!

It was the beginning of seven of the most incredible years of our lives. The River City Good Time Band, born that day, grew into a model program for people with disabilities that would forever raise the standard of expectations for the mentally challenged.

Through the band's performances, we generated enough funds to purchase more than two thousand pounds of musical equipment, choral risers, and lights — and a trailer to haul everything in. With four terrific costume changes, makeup, and styled hair, the confidence level of the students soared. Our expanded group of fourteen band members consistently maintained a repertoire of twenty songs that included solos with background vocals, ensemble singing using two-part harmony, and some show-stopping dance routines. According to the textbooks, this wasn't supposed to be possible.

The River City Good Time Band performed on television and recorded two albums. My six scrapbooks of photos and newspaper clippings document our hundreds of performances in California, Nevada, Utah, Washington, D.C., Denmark, and Iceland.

Dignitaries on the steps of our nation's Capitol marveled at our performance there. A teacher from Sweden came to the stage after one of our concerts in Denmark to say, "You have fulfilled my fondest dream." In Iceland, we sang *Amazing Grace* in a small white church located on that country's most hallowed ground — the place where Vikings converted to Christianity in AD 1000. Following the midnight service, our Icelandic hosts rang the steeple bell ten times, a tribute reserved for honored guests.

Oblivious in the beginning to existing educational practices in regards to music and the mentally challenged, we became cognizant, as we worked with these individuals, of the obvious presence and power of the Lord Jesus Christ. Before every performance, students and parents held hands with us in a prayer circle, asking for God's blessings. The band's second album, "Love of Music Is No Handicap," reflected the heartfelt joy of every member of the group. And those life-changing good times are still influencing others today.

· ·

"For I know the plans I have for you," says the Lord. "They are plans for good and not for disaster, to give you a future and a hope. In those days when you pray, I will listen."

JEREMIAH 29:11–12 NLT

one-finger rule

Vicki Caruana

....

Every act of rebelling expresses a nostalgia for innocence.

ALBERT CAMUS

School dress codes traditionally are a source of discontentment and at times even bring parent lawsuits. (Can you imagine?) Students assume they have "rights" when it comes to what they wear to school. The public schools that require students to wear uniforms or adhere to a strict dress code made the decision knowing they would be taking on a war. I commend them for their willingness to fight. Schools have too often given in to the nonsensical demands of students and their parents. Lack of respect for a dress code is yet one more reason why the authority of teachers has diminished.

Enforcing an appropriate dress code helps ensure the safety of students. With today's record numbers of reported child abuse cases, abductions, and pedophile behavior (add rape — date or otherwise — in or out of school to the list), modest dress can help keep students safe. It does not call attention to itself.

The issue of a school dress code isn't "Who's in charge?" as much as "Who's responsible to keep my child safe in school?" As teachers, we have that responsibility.

How can we enforce a modest dress code on our campuses? Maybe the word *enforce* doesn't adequately describe our task. We must both encourage and expect a modest dress code. The first step is to build trusting relationships with our students. The second is to model this same modesty. And the third is to stay consistent with those expectations.

I know a high school teacher who doubles as the cheerleading coach. Her girls wear the shortest skirts imaginable on the football field. But when it comes to what they wear to school, those girls know and respect Mrs. McVay's one-finger rule. Whether they wear shorts, skirts, or skorts, girls can be sure they are in line with the school's dress code if they let their hands fall to their sides and at least one fingertip touches the hem of their garment. They know they can be stopped at any time during the day to demonstrate whether or not what they're wearing adheres to the one-finger rule. And if it doesn't, well, they have to wear something hideous from the lost and found instead — which contains items still left over from the 1980s.

Mrs. McVay's cheerleaders respect and love her. You can tell she spent a great deal of time building relationships with her girls. One day, when Mrs. McVay and I went to lunch together, one of her cheerleaders came up to us in the restaurant. The girl asked if she could come over to Mrs. McVay's house that night to make sure the new skirt she had purchased met the one-finger rule. She didn't want to take a chance that she would have to wear something from "the box."

Mrs. McVay upheld the school dress code, but she did it with love and grace. As teachers we are upholders of the law — the laws of our schools. We can choose to uphold them as tyrants who rant and rave or as just and gentle rulers who lead conscientiously and with mercy.

If we can encourage others, we should encourage them. If we can give, we should be generous. If we are leaders, we should do our best. If we are good to others, we should do it cheerfully.

ROMANS 12:8 *THE PROMISE*

a teacher, a clown,
and a friend

Karen Allaman

∙∙

*Today's problem student could become tomorrow's leader, and all
because you cared enough to polish that child's mind until the
luster came shining through.*

MARVA COLLINS

*I*t was the fall of 2002, the beginning of a new school
year. As I looked over the list of students assigned to
my fifth grade classroom, there it was — the name I
was looking for, Ron. Ron had quite a reputation in our elementary school. His past was filled with far too much
heartache, and that negatively impacted his behavior. I hoped
to dodge his problems, but there it was — *his* name on *my* list.
That day he became one of my charges, and I began to pray for
him, as I do for all my students.

On the first day of school Ron walked into my classroom
with hair dyed bright red. Looking up, smiling, I said, "Good
morning, Ron! That's one of my favorite shades of red."

I did not get an immediate response, but I noticed a slight upturn in a corner of his mouth, indicating a stifled smile. I immediately decided he had a sense of humor and realized that might be my open door to reaching Ron.

Ron and I developed a routine that included daily bantering and joking around. He rarely looked me or anyone else in the eye, but he was bright and he was funny. He frequently had a story for me, and I shared many jokes with him. I made it my goal to see that upturned corner of his mouth at least once a day. We developed some strategies for talking things out when problems arose, and I felt honored when he decided to confide in me. Eventually, his attendance improved and so did his grades.

The next year I was asked to move to a sixth grade teaching position. I was delighted! I looked forward to spending another year watching these students grow. I was also secretly relieved I had served my time with Ron without a major disruption, and I hoped another one of the sixth grade teachers would find his name on their class list.

In August I received my list, and there was his name again — Ron. I tried not to feel concerned about a bigger, older, preteen Ron. Before long, I realized I had no reason to worry. We started right where we left off, and we both enjoyed the familiarity of my classroom routines. He still struggled socially, and at times academically, but he no longer avoided eye contact with me, and I considered that a real victory. His half smile sometimes broke into full-scale laughter.

At the end of the sixth grade, Ron surprised me with a poem he had written.

> Words alone could never describe the difference you've
> made in my life.
> For two years you've watched me grow,
> Taught me so many things I need to know.
> You're a teacher, a clown, a wife, and a mom.
> You balance it all with grace and charm.
> You support and encourage me in everything I do.
> My life is definitely richer for having known you.
> I will go down many more paths in life it's true.
> But I never would have made it this far without you.
> My time in elementary school has come to an end,
> But I will never forget you, my teacher, my friend.
>
> *Ron*

I was speechless and overcome with emotion. That Ron would take the time to express his feelings and gratitude with a personal tribute overwhelmed me. I keep his poem in my study as a reminder that I can make a difference.

Ron's impact on my life was profound. My life is much richer because of knowing him. I still see Ron occasionally, and he always gives me that crooked smile and says, "Hey, how are you Mrs. A?" It's one of my favorite greetings, and it's a reminder of what God can do when we think our obstacles to effective teaching are too big to handle.

. . . .

*God can do anything, you know — far more than you could
ever imagine or guess or request in your wildest dreams!
He does it not by pushing us around but by working within us,
his Spirit deeply and gently within us.*

EPHESIANS 3:20 MSG

i'll take an "a" for 500, please

Vicki Caruana

*We know nothing about motivation.
All we can do is write books about it.*

PETER DRUCKER

*T*hose who teach middle school students are sometimes called crazy. You have to be a little crazy to love preteens with their raging hormones and changing bodies. I loved teaching sixth grade because they still loved learning and thought well of their teachers. They always reminded me of deer caught in headlights with their wide eyes and naïve expectations. Seventh graders are . . . well . . . different.

Seventh graders are the stepchildren of middle school. They think they know everything, when in reality they know very little. They are full of bravado and question authority as often as possible. They speak before thinking, and they drive parents and teachers crazy with their insistence that things be done their way. They approach school like a flea market, trying to bargain their way through their classes. What is the least amount of work they can do to get the grade that they want? Seventh graders like to haggle.

"What will you give me for doing that?" was the question posed to me when I assigned the first book report of the year. This was not a question I was prepared to answer. It caught me by surprise. It made me wonder who had promised them anything in the past to make them expect something from me as well.

"If we finish our work, can we watch a movie?"

"Can't I just type my final report now and skip the rough draft?"

"Do we get extra credit if we finish on time?"

The challenge to motivate students seems to occupy much of my time and energy. I often think, *If I could just get into their hearts, I know I could get through to them*. But when education seems to have a price tag on it, I realize that I can't *make* kids want to learn for the sake of learning. I can only hope they will care enough to try to excel. And I want them to excel!

It wasn't until I was in graduate school that I realized the power of expectations. One of my professors told us that he expected to see only A's and B's from the class. He defined in great detail what we must do to get a B and what we must to do to get an A. He didn't expect lower than a B, so he never defined a C, D, or F. Basically, we chose our grades and worked to secure them. I wondered if this approach would work with my seventh graders.

To my amazement, the first time I tried this approach, a fourth of my students jumped at the chance to work for an A. Three-fourths chose to work for a B. But by the end of the school year, more than 80 percent of my students actually achieved higher grades than they had the previous quarter. The responsibility had shifted from the teacher *giving* them grades to students *claiming* their grades. They had taken ownership of their own education.

I thought I could only get to the hearts from the inside out, but working from the outside in worked just as well. I didn't have to force them to work. I didn't have to haggle over grades. I just offered them a different set of choices. It was a win-win situation for all of us. We get what we expect. Mix high expectations with encouragement and you end up with a class full of achievers.

God's expectations of us are pretty high. He doesn't haggle over the price of our salvation. But he offers us encouragement and companionship along the way. We can do the same for our students.

* * *

Teach your children to choose the right path,
and when they are older, they will remain upon it.

PROVERBS 22:6 NLT

believe it!

Bonnie Afman Emmorey

....

Experience teaches only the teachable.

ALDOUS HUXLEY

*U*p and down the school hallway, you could hear the kids talking. "You won't believe what Mrs. Emmorey has on today!"

It was true. I had a dramatic flair, and when it came to my teaching wardrobe, I had fun. I regularly wore wild and crazy clothes. I figured that as long as the students had to look at me all day, my clothing might as well be entertaining — from palazzo pants and oriental tunics, to sashes and turbans, and everything in between. I enjoyed making a visual splash. From the time I was teenager, I was drawn to the unusual, and now that I was a substitute teacher, my unusual clothing was a way of connecting with the students on a different level.

However, it wasn't until I taught public school sex education — the *talk* about Mrs. Emmorey *really* started! It was a tenth grade, mixed gender health class, and halfway through the scheduled movie, I knew I couldn't stay silent. I was shocked at the misinformation given as fact. The movie was encouraging "safe sex" as a viable means of enjoying relationships while controlling potential pregnancy and disease.

As a Christian, I was teaching my own sons that abstinence until marriage was the biblical and morally correct choice. We had just recently had the *big talk* with Nathan, our oldest son, and it was an event to remember. Nate was in the fourth grade and growing more and more curious about the birds and the bees.

One Sunday afternoon, I looked at Nathan and said, "Nate, tell Dad to turn off the game. It's time to talk." As a fifth grade teacher, my husband, Ron, was prepared for handling this important discussion that would prepare our son for adolescence. A half hour after their conversation began, I walked in to give the woman's perspective. Ron had just finished and I heard him say, "Nathan, if you have any questions, come to your mom or me. If you ask one of your friends, you might not get an honest answer, but we will always tell you the truth."

The floodgates opened! Nate must have been storing up questions in anticipation of this discussion. Ron and I had a hard time controlling our laughter at his first query.

"Dad, I understand about the mating process, but how do you know when you're done?"

"You'll know, son, you'll know," came Ron's quick response.

"How often do you *do* it?" The next question was asked with barely a pause.

"As often as possible." Again, I saw my husband stifling his laughter.

Nathan's list of questions was not exhausted. "I know you said Mom can't have any more babies — so why do you still *do* it?"

Ron was ready with the answer. "Because it's *fun*."

Our talk with Nathan was running through my head as I watched the sex education video that day. I was deeply concerned about the information presented as factual to these impressionable teenagers — and *I* was the person responsible for the teaching that followed the movie. How could I possibly let the students leave the classroom and not tell them the truth? They needed to know there is no such thing as "safe sex."

As the video ended, I flipped on the light switch. I could see embarrassment on the faces. No one quite knew where to look. It was time to take a risk and take action.

"That was a very interesting video, but you were not given the whole picture. Before I say anything more, I'd like to show you pictures of my two sons, Nathan and his younger brother, Jordan. Pass Jordan's picture around, because he was conceived with 'safe sex.'"

An audible gasp was heard. What had Mrs. Emmorey said?

Quietly, I explained that my husband, Ron, and I had *planned* a longer span of time between our children. When a condom broke, *our* time plan failed, and Jordan was conceived.

For our family, he was not a child born out of wedlock, but into a family that was excited to have another child. When it happened, we rejoiced.

Oh my, how the news spread! When I entered the teachers' lounge later that day, the conversation stopped and I was informed that the school hallways were ringing with the news. "You won't believe what Mrs. Emmorey said!" No longer were my flamboyant outfits the talk of the school or of the teachers' lounge. The word spread and soon everyone in our small town knew what I taught the students in health class. That day I shared something I had never spoken aloud before, but I knew it needed to be said.

My sons are now in their twenties, and I will be forever grateful that *my* attempt at "safe sex" failed. And, believe it or not, maybe I helped some tenth graders in public school make wiser choices. It was worth the risk.

. . . .

He who trusts in himself is a fool,
but he who walks in wisdom is kept safe.

PROVERBS 28:26

most likely to . . .

Vicki Caruana

Teachers can change lives with just the right mix of chalk and challenges.

Joyce A. Myers

B y the time I graduated from high school they had stopped the yearbook tradition of putting adjectives under the names of graduating seniors. I was disappointed because I couldn't wait to see what they would say about me. They might have said, "Musical, a good friend, smart, redhead." Our graduating class was huge — 950 students! There were just too many of us for individual attention in the yearbook. Yet, it would have been nice.

Over the years I've calculated that I probably have come in contact with approximately eight hundred students. I taught for only seven years, so I know that most teachers have touched the lives of many more students than I have. Some of those students left us without notice. Others, for good or bad, left permanent memories. Even now as I look in my old yearbooks from my teaching days, I fill in those adjectives about certain students.

Fun-loving, popular, smart. Dramatic, involved, student council president. These were the obvious, the noticed, and the known.

Then there were those who either weren't noticed or who were noticed for the wrong reasons. Their adjectives wouldn't be included in any yearbook because they weren't positive. As teachers we thought them just the same.

Desperate, angry, worked below potential. Depressed, quiet, withdrawn. Struggling, frustrated, left behind. We noticed these students, but I often wonder how many of us did more than just notice them.

I remember looking at certain students and saying to myself, "Most likely to end up in jail or worse." Those were the students who consumed my thoughts, who invaded my dreams, and for whom I prayed more than I did for the others.

Anne, a high school teacher, has had more than her share of these kinds of students. She told me a story about a young man who, despite her prayers and attention, did end up in jail. Their paths crossed more than once over the next few years. Then ten years passed before she saw him again, this time on the school grounds.

"What are you doing here?" she asked.

"I'm working for the roofing company that's putting on the school's new roof," he said. He searched her face for signs of acceptance.

"That's wonderful. It seems you are turning your life around." Anne was pleased.

"I'm trying to. This job is actually part of the work-release program," he said. A bit of disappointment flashed across Anne's face, and her former student saw it.

"I wanted to stop by and see you. I wanted you, of all people, to see that I'm on the right path now."

Anne remembered all the times she had pushed this boy to be better than his environment. He remembered her persistence and depended on it. Anne was proud of him and she told him so.

The next morning there were flowers waiting for her on her desk. They were from *him*. The card said, "I'm still alive because of you. Thank you for always thinking the best of me."

What adjectives do we silently attach to our students? Success isn't always measured by career or status in the community. Our expectations as teachers can shape the future for our students. With our help, students who struggle now can still become the ones who are "most likely to succeed." Our hope is in God, who is the changer of hearts.

Why are you downcast, O my soul? Why so disturbed within me? Put your hope in God, for I will yet praise him, my Savior and my God.

PSALM 42:11

a medal around his neck

Phyllis Harmony

....

And as our love expands, so our whole personality will grow, slowly but truly. Every fresh soul we touch in love is going to teach us something fresh about God.

Evelyn Underhill

When I picked up the phone, I couldn't tell if I was hearing laughing or crying, and at first I wasn't able to identify the caller. "Hello, who is it? What's wrong?"

I finally realized it was my sister. She took a deep breath and sighed. "Oh, Phyllis, I knew it would happen someday, but I never dreamed it would be in the first grade."

I instantly knew she was referring to her son, my precious nephew Josh. Josh has a condition called Fragile X, associated with autism. "Peggy, tell me what happened." My eyes welled up with tears. My sister had received a call from the teacher explaining that during recess three of Josh's classmates talked him into doing something very inappropriate. Later in the afternoon the teacher left the room for a few minutes and the same boys talked Josh into repeating his earlier actions for the class.

A little girl told the teacher about the incident as soon as she returned. Devastated, the teacher hauled the three boys to the principal's office and called my sister with the report. After questioning the boys, the principal determined that their goading of Josh was for no other reason than to make fun of him and his special needs. Josh, however, with his limited comprehension, thought the boys were just being friendly.

That evening as Peggy shared the details with her husband, Joe, they decided the boys needed to be taught a helpful lesson. It was challenging to try to figure out how to explain the negative impact their behavior could have on someone else. After a lot of discussion and sincere prayer, Josh's parents had an idea that could work for the whole class of first graders.

Joe and Peggy made arrangements with the teacher to come in and talk with the class about kids with special needs while Josh was being tutored in another room. When they arrived, they set some items on the teacher's desk. First, they held up a bowl. "Imagine this bowl full of vanilla ice cream. Doesn't that sound good?" Peggy asked.

"Oh, yes!" the little voices cried out.

Next they held up a bottle of chocolate sauce. "Now imagine pouring this sauce all over the ice cream. What will it do for the ice cream?" Joe asked.

The wide-eyed first graders shouted out over each other, "It will make it even better!"

"That's right," Joe and Peggy affirmed. Then they held up a bottle of hot pepper sauce. "Now imagine putting this sauce on the ice cream," they said.

The kids screamed, "No! That will ruin the ice cream! Yuck!"

"Just like that bowl of ice cream, we are all likable," Peggy explained. "We also have the choice to add good things or bad things to each other, just like putting the good and bad sauces on the ice cream."

"Our choices," Joe added, "could make something better or worse."

Putting aside the ice cream, they explained Josh's medical condition as well as they could to a first grade audience. Then they answered questions from the children.

In the coming days, this instruction seemed to produce a favorable result. There was no more taking advantage of Josh for the purpose of amusement.

A few weeks later Josh participated in his first Special Olympics. I watched him win his first three medals. He wore them proudly around his neck. The following week at school, he had a chance to tell the students about his medals and how he won them. As he stood in front of his class, a hand went up in the back. "Josh, could I try on your medal?" a little girl asked.

"Why sure, Bethany, come on up." Bethany came to the front of the class. Josh took off one of his medals, placed it around her neck, stood back looking at her, and then announced, "Let's everyone clap for Bethany for having the prettiest red shoes in the class." Everyone clapped.

Another hand went up, "Josh, can I try on your medal?"

With a big smile Josh said, "Sure, Brandon, come on up." He placed a medal around Brandon's neck, stood back, and said, "Let's everyone clap for Brandon for having the most freckles." And the clapping went on. One by one, every child in the class came forward and wore one of the medals while Josh found a reason for the class to applaud them.

I want a heart like Josh has. I want a heart that sees something good in everyone, even those who have hurt me. Josh put the effort into winning the medals and then shared the medals with everyone while finding a reason to make each one feel significant. The other students didn't have to do a thing but ask to wear his medal.

Then it struck me. That's what Jesus did for me. He freely gave his all — his life — on the cross. He gladly shares his love with me, finding me significant enough to be the recipient of his love and forgiveness — and all I have to do is ask for it.

....

But God made our bodies with many parts, and he has put each part just where he wants it. If one part suffers, all the parts suffer with it, and if one part is honored, all the parts are glad. Now all of you together are Christ's body, and each one of you is a separate and necessary part of it.

1 Corinthians 12:18, 26–27 NLT

high school rivals

Vicki Caruana

. . . .

People are usually more firmly convinced that their opinions are precious than that they are true.

GEORGE SANTAYANA

igh school rivalry didn't affect me personally until after I graduated. When I found out where I would gain my student teaching experience, I cringed. Largo High School had always been a formidable opponent in sporting events, but it was their reputation as scoundrels that made them seem much more dreadful. Our school felt superior in every way. But behind our backs we were called Seminole Snobs. Looking back, I believe the name fit.

I certainly felt like a snob as I walked from the parking lot into the old Largo building. I caught myself more than once shaking my head in disgust at the dingy hallways and much-in-need-of-painting lockers. The first time I entered the teachers' lounge I felt as if I were in enemy territory. I was convinced everyone was looking at me and mocking me, somehow already knowing I was from Seminole. Of course, they weren't, but perception is everything.

My first week at Largo High School was surprisingly uneventful. Although I felt like a traitor spending time in that school, I secretly began to feel a sense of belonging. Everyone was so nice to me, even after they found out I was a Seminole! One teacher put it this way, "Well, at least you've got your health. That's all that matters." These teachers were more accepting, more supportive than I could ever have expected. I wondered if they were really the scoundrels we thought they were. The days of high school rivalry were behind me. Or so I thought.

Six weeks into my internship I had the chance to talk to teachers from my own alma mater at a district workshop. Many were the same teachers I had when I went to school there. At first they were thrilled that I was going into teaching. They even suggested that I try to get a job at their school. Then I told them where I was student teaching. Big mistake!

"Lousy school. I can't believe the university put you there."

"How can you stand it? I'll bet you're counting the days."

"Don't worry. We'll put in a good word for you here. Then you'll teach at a top-notch school."

On and on it went. All I could think about were the teachers and students back at *my* school. They didn't deserve this slander. *My* school? When had it become my school? Suddenly all I wanted to do was leave that workshop and drive back to where I felt I belonged — at my rival high school!

Sitting in that workshop with those teachers, I felt like a fraud. I didn't agree with their assessment of my student teaching school. I knew that silence meant agreement.

"Actually, I'm having a great time. The teachers were welcoming and helpful."

All other conversation at our table stopped.

"You mean you like it there?" my former social studies teacher asked.

"I do," I said with initial hesitation. "And if they offer me a job when I'm finished with my student teaching, I would be honored to accept." I finished with more bravado than I felt.

They were speechless. Then again, I didn't stick around long enough to hear what else they had to say. It made me wonder who the real enemy was.

* * *

Let me not be put to shame, O Lord, for I have cried out to you; but let the wicked be put to shame and lie silent in the grave. Let their lying lips be silenced, for with pride and contempt they speak arrogantly against the righteous.

PSALM 31:17 – 18

virtual reunion

Vicki Caruana

. . . .

*The deepest principle in human nature is the craving
to be appreciated.*

WILLIAM JAMES

The Internet has opened up the world and made it accessible to everyone with a computer. Personally, I don't know what I would do without it. We moved around a lot when I was growing up, and the Internet has allowed me to find people I cared about from that time. It's always fun to click on a reunion site or a place such as *class-mates.com* to look for long-lost friends. I have found quite a few and have reconnected with some very special people.

When you think about someone from your past, do you ever wonder if they think of you as well? I've been pleasantly surprised to find out that they do! Yes, you can look up an old boyfriend. Yes, you can find your best friend from kindergarten. Guess what? You can find your old teachers, too. I found one of mine just recently.

Mrs. Carole Kurtz was my third grade teacher in Old Bridge, New Jersey, in the early 1970s. I was in the same class with Cori, one of her daughters. Mrs. Kurtz was elegant, creative, and encouraging. I remember that we had "free" reading time each day. It was my favorite part of the day. She allowed us to sit anywhere we wanted to read: at our desks, under our desks, even in the coat closet (my personal favorite). She had so many books in her classroom that I rarely felt the need to check one out of the school library.

Mrs. Kurtz also exposed us to traditional topics in nontraditional ways. When we studied the pioneer days during history, we learned to churn butter and make our own candles. We learned about the stock market by buying and selling shares in a classroom market that she created. We built radios, batteries, and a virtual V-6 engine during science. Mrs. Kurtz was ahead of her time. She was creative and fearless, I wanted to be just like her.

I found Cori Kurtz online this past year. It was fun catching up with one another. Then I asked about her mom. I found out where Mrs. Kurtz was living. The greatest surprise was that she was online, too! Cori graciously reintroduced us and I was finally able to tell Mrs. Kurtz how much she meant to me.

"You can call me Carole," she instant-messaged me.

"No, I can't," I said. "You are still Mrs. Kurtz to me."

She was thrilled to hear from me. She humbly accepted my praise of her. As a teacher I know how much it means to hear from a former student. The rewards of teaching can continue well into retirement.

If you haven't taken the time to thank the teacher who made a difference in your life, don't wait. For some of us it may be too late. They may have already left us. But it's worth the effort to search. You never know. Send an email. When your former teacher's computer says, "You've got mail!" it may be just what that teacher needs that day — to hear from *you*. Every little "thank you" is a blessing from God. To whom can you be a blessing today?

* *

Be joyful always; pray continually; give thanks in all circumstances, for this is God's will for you in Christ Jesus.

1 THESSALONIANS 5:16

a girl called cricket

Cathy Gallagher

· ·

There is always one moment in childhood when the door opens and lets the future in.

GRAHAM GREENE

he smudge-faced urchins standing in the doorway could have come off the pages of Catherine Marshall's *Christy*. The boy, about six years old, was holding tight to the hand of a girl I guessed was four. He wore an over-sized, tattered jacket and a narrow-brimmed cap pulled low on his forehead. She wore a faded, crumpled, puff-sleeved dress. Stringy strands of dull blonde hair brushed her fragile-looking shoulders.

The boy's eyes darted around the room and locked on mine. He asked, "You the teacher?"

"Yes," I said.

"My sister's Cricket. The preacher said this is 'er class. I'll be back to git 'er."

Glancing in his sister's direction, he said, "Wait for me, Cricket. Ya hear?"

An unpleasant, pungent odor began to fill the room. Cricket nodded and looked at me through huge, round, pleading eyes. I helped her find a seat around the table with six other children. The odor followed her into the room, growing stronger. I wondered, *How will the children react to the smell? What will I do if they are mean to her?* The children, however, seemed not to notice, and I wondered if they were breathing through their mouths like I was. I wished I could dab a perfume-dipped handkerchief underneath my nose to mask the odor, like Catherine Marshall's Christy had done.

I was a first-time, seventeen-year-old Sunday school teacher. I had envisioned a classroom filled with well-scrubbed, well-dressed, sweet-smelling children as I filled my first lesson plan with fun activities. Cricket did not fit that image.

That Sunday, Cricket didn't say much, but her eyes didn't miss a thing. She listened intently, and she and the others had fun getting to know each other while completing their Bible lesson activities.

Cricket's brother dropped her off at my classroom door every Sunday. One day I asked if Cricket was her given name. He answered, "Name's Ruth. Goes by Cricket." I thought about Ruth's story in the Bible. How fitting a name for this gentle, respectful, loving, doe-eyed child. As the weeks went by, the children never mentioned the overpowering odor surrounding Cricket, which surprised me.

One Sunday Cricket burst into the room shouting, "Teacher! Teacher! Look what I brung ya!" She opened her small, grease-coated, patent-leather purse and spilled grayish-colored popcorn onto the table.

Gulp. Smile. "Thank you, honey!" I said as I looked her in the eyes and gave her a big hug. She was so excited about doing something nice for me.

That Sunday Cricket's eyes lit up and her face glowed as we talked about where Jesus lives and how much Jesus loves all little children. My heart melted when Cricket patted her heart and, with dancing eyes, said, "Oh, Teacher! I love Jesus, too."

The next three Sundays, Cricket was absent. Worried, I decided to make a home visit. The pastor and two church leaders met me as I was leaving church. They said they had met with Cricket's mother three weeks earlier, telling her that the children had to be clean and odor-free to come to Sunday school.

Anger filled my heart. Tears filled my eyes. *Was this why she stopped coming?* The children in my class had not complained or been mean or disrespectful. I sputtered, "How could you? When Jesus said, 'Suffer the little children to come onto me,' he never said they had to be clean!" I stomped off to tell my mother what had happened.

Later my mother drove me to Cricket's home. I knocked on the door. No one answered. A neighbor said the family had moved, address unknown. My heart sank. I would never know if she stopped coming because of what the church leaders told her mother or because the family needed to move. I longed to hug her and tell her that Jesus and I loved her.

I still think about the doe-eyed, gentle beauty called Cricket, who loved Jesus and who captured my heart on my first day as a teenaged Sunday school teacher forty years ago. It was a teaching experience that will stay with me for a lifetime — and one that reinforced what I know about Jesus' view of children.

<hr />

"Don't push these children away. Don't ever get between them and me. These children are at the very center of life in the kingdom. Mark this: Unless you accept God's kingdom in the simplicity of a child, you'll never get in." Then, gathering the children up in his arms, he laid his hands of blessing on them.

MARK 10:14–16 MSG

forever young

Vicki Caruana

. . . .

Nothing great was ever achieved without enthusiasm.

EMERSON

When our youngest child was beginning kindergarten, I didn't know much about the teachers at his school. The word was that Mrs. Sexton was the best kindergarten teacher. She was full of enthusiasm, yet maintained discipline. She loved teaching and she loved kids. I decided Mrs. Sexton was the best choice for Charles. I turned in a brief but expectant letter to the principal in hopes that he would place my son with the best.

He did.

But she turned out to be older — much older — than I expected.

By the time she taught my son, Molly Sexton had taught for thirty-two years. When I found this nugget of insider information, I contemplated whether it was worth upsetting the apple cart (so to speak) and request a different teacher. How could someone still have enthusiasm after all those years? Charles was already reluctant to go to school. I didn't want him discouraged by a seasoned teacher — one seasoned with vim and vinegar instead of sweetness and spice. Finally, though, I chose not to make waves and left the assignment as it was. And boy, was I glad I did.

I knew Mrs. Sexton was a pro from the first day I stepped into her classroom. Her room was one of the most inviting classrooms I had ever been in. Not too busy with over-decoration. Not sterile like many high school classrooms. It was just right. She welcomed each and every child as if their class was her very first class. For my son, it was love at first sight. I knew it would be a good year when he slipped his hand out of mine and followed Mrs. Sexton to the activity center without looking back. I stood there, mesmerized by her confidence and her grace. I wanted to linger, but knew it was better for Charles if I didn't.

I once asked Molly Sexton what kept her going. "Loving these little ones as my own makes all the difference," she said. "And remembering how much their parents love them helps when they're driving me crazy!"

Nine hundred students and their parents later, Molly reminisced about her own growth as a teacher. "I still don't know it all," she explained. "I still have a lot to learn and I pray that I learn what I need when I need it."

All of those years of teaching helped her to quickly see the light inside each child put in her care. It was as if she cherished the time she had with them. But even with all that experience, she treated each child as an individual and drew out of them the best they had to offer. They wanted to please her. They wanted to linger. Leaving a teacher you love, even to advance to the next grade, seems both unnecessary and even painful to some children. Charles wanted Mrs. Sexton to be his teacher forever and for always. That is the greatest compliment a teacher can receive.

In the minds of our students, we are still the same as when they sat in our classes. We are, therefore, forever young. Look at yourself through their eyes, aged as they may be now, and recapture for yourself the enthusiasm and dedication you had long ago. Decide to grow into a seasoned teacher — seasoned with all the ingredients of a teacher they will never forget. And when you are faced with the prospect of working with a veteran teacher, honor him or her with the respect they have earned.

A wise teacher's words spur students to action and emphasize important truths. The collected sayings of the wise are like guidance from a shepherd.

Ecclesiastes 12:11 NLT

roses are red, violets are blue

Vicki Caruana

. . . .

I can live for two months on a good compliment.

MARK TWAIN

J have two sets of yearbooks — the ones from when I
was in school and the others from when I taught in
school. I remember what a thrill it was to get a
teacher to sign my yearbook. They always said things like
"Good luck to a nice student next year!" Well, I know that's not
a life-changing note of encouragement, but somehow it meant
a lot to me. You could never trust what your "friends" would
write, or people you thought were your friends. Their notes
were more like, "Roses are red, violets are blue, if I had your
hair, I'd be sad and blue!" I have red hair, and growing up I was
the only one in my class with red hair. It was a source of constant teasing and torturous remarks.

When I became a teacher, I was pleasantly surprised to
discover that many of my students wanted me to sign their

yearbooks. (I asked them to sign mine as well.) What surprised me most was that students I had the most difficulty with also wanted me to sign their yearbooks.

I was painfully aware of the importance of those little encouraging notes. I wanted to do more than say, "Good luck next year!" It was a challenge to come up with something encouraging to write without sounding preachy. One boy in particular was a regular cut-up in class. He frequently challenged my authority, as if his mission in life was to disrupt class time. The thing of it was, he was pretty funny. More than once I had to turn my back so he wouldn't see me laughing. It was like when your two-year-old says "No!" to you with his pouty lips and chubby cheeks, stamping his foot with his hands on his hips. You know you should reprimand him for being defiant and saying no, but he is just too darn cute! That's what it was like with Larry.

As he waited for me to write in his yearbook, I decided to give him a gift.

Dear Larry,

I wish you only the best as you go to high school. I have to admit . . . you made me laugh. Thank you for that.

When Larry read what I had written, he didn't look at me. He was speechless. Now *that* was a first! As he started to leave my desk, he turned back at the last moment and hugged me.

That was the last time I saw Larry. I hope that wherever he is now, he is making people laugh. It's a gift.

··

Blessed are the merciful, for they will be shown mercy. Blessed are the pure in heart, for they will see God. Blessed are the peacemakers, for they will be called sons of God.

MATTHEW 5:7–9

mission impossible!

Carol Kent

Education is leading human souls to what is best, and making what is best out of them.

John Ruskin

*J*t was the spring of 1975. Seven months earlier two important events took place in my life — I completed my master's degree and one month later I gave birth to my first child, Jason Paul. Since my baby's due date was in mid-October, it seemed wise to take a sabbatical from teaching and devote myself to being a stay-at-home mom.

I loved being a mom, but it was harder than I thought. Having taught junior high speech, drama, and English for the past four years, I agonized over wanting to be a great mother, but also over my longing to reach young learners. My students had honored me with the "Teacher of the Year" award before I left, and I missed them. I also missed the numerous opportunities I had to share my faith with students during non-classroom hours in our little town where "everybody knows everybody."

One day the phone rang. It was my public school superintendent. "Carol, we have an opening in the alternative education program for pregnant teenagers." He went on: "Your job would be to individualize high school academic subjects so pregnant girls in our county could stay in school during the duration of their pregnancies and for the first few months following the birth of their babies. You would also coordinate instruction in nutrition, life skills, and basic mothering techniques. Would you be interested in interviewing for this position?"

Would I be interested? I could hardly hold my enthusiasm in check long enough to respond in a professional manner. "Oh, sir," I exuded, "I would love to be considered for this job!" The position was offered to me during the first interview, and a young couple from my church volunteered to care for my son during school hours. They lived only a few blocks away from the Project 23 house where I would be teaching the girls in the program, beginning in September. "Project 23" was our affectionate name for the home, which was owned by the school. Two numbers — "2" and "3" — hung precariously near the front door, and since our program was definitely a "project," thus, the name: Project 23.

Saying yes to this position was a first step, but facing the intimidating responsibility of the job brought a rude awakening. I wondered how any teacher could be labeled as "successful" with such a diverse group of students who needed individualized curriculum on multiple grade levels. The mission was challenging, but it also felt like I was climbing Mt. Everest without either the proper equipment or a guide.

Over a two-year period sixty-eight pregnant teenagers passed through the program. During my final year, seven students were fourteen years old.

The comments of my students were sometimes shocking, often surprising, and at times gut-wrenching. Many didn't know for sure who fathered their baby. A few said they planned their current pregnancy because they had aborted their first child and felt so guilty about destroying a life, they had to replace it. Their comments revealed thoughts, longings, and struggles:

"Being a mom is harder than I thought. Babies don't just eat and sleep; they cry a lot."

"My mom and dad hate me for being a disgrace to our family, but I don't care. I hate them, too."

"I wonder if anyone will ever want to marry me. If a guy marries me, he gets a kid, too."

Hailey came into my life during my first year at Project 23. She was different from the others. She was a straight-A student and had been captain of the cheerleading squad before her pregnancy became known. Her boyfriend, Josh, was the quarterback on the football team. She confided in me that her parents had high hopes for her future success, and she knew they were disappointed in her. She said, "I blew it! I know Josh cares more about the fall football season than he cares about this baby and me, but I really want to be a good mom. We may end up getting married eventually, but we're too young for that right now."

Hailey and other students often stayed after class to talk, and I frequently had my eighteen-month-old son, Jason, at the Project 23 house after school hours. My husband would stop by and banter with the girls, so both of us got to know the students well. In time, my fears about teaching this diverse group of students dissipated. I prayed for them by name and asked God to help me make a difference in their lives.

One day Hailey said, "Mrs. Kent, do you know the most important thing I've learned from you?" I was expecting her to tell me how much she appreciated the hard work I had done to keep her up to speed academically so she could graduate with her class.

"What's that?" I asked.

"You've shown me how to be a loving mom. I've watched the way you hold your son and talk to him, as if he's the most important person in your life. I've watched your relationship with your husband, too. I see the way he looks at you and respects you. He cherishes you and he's proud of you. I want a husband who treats me like that. I've learned more about what I want out of life through observing you and your family than I have from anything else you taught in our school this year. Thanks."

As the year ended, I watched Hailey make the difficult decision to become a single mom while she waited for an immature teenaged football player to grow up. I felt a deep sense of gratitude to God. In the beginning, my mission seemed impossible — educating teenagers who were in the middle of major transitions, relationship struggles, and the stresses of pregnancy and motherhood. He revealed the best way I could teach my students was to live my Christian life in an authentic way, without being preachy or pushy. The students needed to trust me before they could open their minds to learning.

* * *

I was unsure of how to go about this, and felt totally inadequate — I was scared to death, if you want the truth of it — and so nothing I said could have impressed you or anyone else. But the Message came through anyway. God's Spirit and God's power did it, which made it clear that your life of faith is a response to God's power, not to some fancy mental or emotional footwork by me or anyone else.

1 CORINTHIANS 2:4–5 MSG

gullible jane

Vicki Caruana

....

We are all here on earth to help others; what on earth the others are here for I don't know.

W. H. AUDEN

Quite often I travel to school districts to present inspirational workshops during their in-service training. Recently, during one back-to-school workshop, I asked the audience to come up with four ways they could do something nice for those in their school without being asked.

The answers are usually pretty similar from school to school:

- First one in the building turns on the heat or air conditioning.
- Take someone else's duty for a day.
- Bring donuts (or other delectables).
- Remember birthdays.
- First one in the building makes the coffee.

Jane thought this was a wonderful activity. You could tell that she was a person always looking to please those around her.

But Jane was also known as gullible. She took seriously even the most adolescent comments, but she did it with a smile. If you were having a bad day, a visit to Jane would surely cheer you up. Jane told the group about an experience from her first year at their school.

On her first day, the principal told her what was expected of her. One expectation was that she should bring in donuts every Friday for the staff and faculty. Jane, always aiming to please — and taking everything everyone said to heart — brought in donuts every Friday for the entire school year! Her principal was just kidding. However, he saw no reason to let her in on that fact.

Even when Jane discovered that she had been on the receiving end of a practical joke, she continued to bring in the donuts. She didn't get angry or feel bad about herself for being so gullible; she took it in stride. She liked seeing her colleagues enjoy those donuts every Friday. It made them happy. It made the school a happier place to teach. That made Jane happy, too.

Can we be vulnerable enough with one another to look for ways to please one another? Can we trust that God will protect our most gullible souls? God is praised when we smile. We are blessed when he smiles. I encourage you to bring some unexpected happiness to your school. Remember, teachers are cheap dates — we are happy with donuts every time!

* * *

Blessed are the pure in heart, for they will see God.
MATTHEW 5:8

dancing scarecrows

Karen Allaman

There are people who, instead of listening to what is being said to them, are already listening to what they are going to say themselves.

ALBERT GUINON

*J*ason's words "I can't" echoed in my mind as I gazed at his scarecrow, which was displayed on the bulletin board outside our first grade classroom. The board was filled with twenty-one purple and orange dancing autumn scarecrows. As I cleaned up the last of the cookies and punch from our back-to-school parent night, my mind drifted back to the day we made those scarecrows and to what I learned by listening to Jason.

Armed with sharpened pencils and blunt-edged scissors, the students waited patiently as I passed them patterns for a sixteen-piece scarecrow art project. They started tracing and cutting with quiet determination. As the snipping and clipping reached a frantic pace, the floor was littered with random scarecrow parts and the desks were covered with partially clad, frightful figures.

My classroom resembled a scarecrow body parts store, and I had the daunting task of taking inventory and arranging products!

With glue bottles in hand, the assembly process began. I was surprised to see children place their scarecrow's eyes closer to the scarecrow's mouth than the forehead. Several scarecrows' hands were glued to their shoulders, and arms and legs were stuck on in unbelievable contortions! There was more glue on the children than there was on the scarecrows, and there were more questions and pleas for help than I could possibly answer.

In an effort to bring some organization to this cornfield massacre, I said, "Children, turn your scarecrow over and write your first and last name on the back so you are sure to get your own scarecrow back at the end of Parent Night."

Jason's hand went up and he said, "Mrs. Allaman, I can't!"

"Jason, it's okay if you can't remember how to write your last name. Just put your initials on the back of your scarecrow." I continued reassembling anatomically incorrect scarecrows.

Again, Jason's hand was waving in the air, this time with more persistence. "Mrs. Allaman, I can't!"

I impatiently replied, "I know you can write a J, it looks like this." I made a big fish hook in the air and turned away.

I glued a nose on the face of a scarecrow, mended torn scarecrow limbs, and unglued children's fingers. I looked around to see what else needed to be done when I saw Jason's head on his desk. He was sobbing into his arms, shaking his head back and forth, saying *over and over*, "I can't! I can't!"

Trying hard not to show my frustration, I said, "What do you mean, you *can't*, Jason? I know you can make a J."

When I finally gave Jason my full attention, he calmed down enough to explain. Through his tears he sniffled, "I know how to write my name, but I can't turn over my scarecrow. I think I used too much glue. I can't turn it over!" He sobbed into my shoulder as I tried to comfort him.

He was right; he couldn't turn over his scarecrow. Neither could I. It was glued fast to his desk. I had to use a spatula to scrape it off. It took forty-five minutes to get the excess glue off the desk and repair the damaged scarecrow.

Jason's scarecrow was salvaged, but I knew I was not going to be an effective teacher if I caused my students such unnecessary frustration. I realized *listening* was a skill I needed to develop.

I learned a lot about classroom organization and preparation that day. But I learned far more from Jason about an important skill, a gift we can give to our students, a necessary skill for effective teachers — listening — *really* listening.

* * *

Post this at all the intersections, dear friends:
Lead with your ears, follow up with your tongue.

JAMES 1:19 MSG

about me

Vicki Caruana

. . . .

Even if we can't be happy, we must always be cheerful.

Irving Kristol

*T*eaching is all about relationship. The best teachers take the time to get to know individual students: their learning styles, their wants and dreams, their family life, and the rest of their life outside the classroom. But relationship-building is a two-way street. It can be difficult to get to know twenty or more students. Students have the advantage. They only have to get to know one teacher (okay, sometimes more).

As teachers we sometimes make our lives outside the classroom seem mysterious and opaque. That's why our students' jaws drop when they see us in the grocery store or at the mall. It occurs to them, maybe for the first time, that we are real people with real lives outside of school. It tickles them to see us with our spouses or children. We hope they won't see us exit an R-rated movie or an establishment that serves liquor. We wouldn't want to tarnish the image they have of us. But there's something to be said for revealing the real inner person in measured doses. It can level the playing field just enough for them to trust us.

One of my favorite things to do as a teacher was to create an "About Me" bulletin board. It included things like my class photos through elementary school, my senior photo, my college diploma, samples of my school work at certain ages, photos of my family, and so forth. Students found great pleasure in finding me in my school photos, although it wasn't that difficult since I was usually the only redhead in my class.

The "About Me" board accomplished two things. First, it showed my students that I, indeed, had a past—one that was much like their own, one to which they could easily relate. Second, it reminded me why I do what I do. Looking at my own class photos made me smile. I liked school. Watching my students giggle and point and sometimes quietly ponder was all the inspiration I needed to keep teaching—especially on those days when I wondered why I was still there.

Someone once said, "When the teacher sneezes, all of her students catch a cold!" Happiness is contagious too, especially when we build close relationships with our students.

* *

All the days of the oppressed are wretched, but the cheerful heart has a continual feast.

PROVERBS 15:15

a shaping lesson

Melissa S. Sutter

....

*Some of us want to be with the crowd so badly
that we end up in a mess.*

CHARLES SWINDOLL

She was one of my students — seventeen, sweet, and cute. As she read her report in front of the class, her brilliant smile lit up the room. Bethany's classmates seemed captivated with every word she spoke. I was amazed. Never before had I witnessed anything quite like this.

I wish I could tell you the topic on which Bethany spoke. But, to be honest, I can't remember a single word she said. What I do remember are the reactions and words of her classmates.

Brian whispered loudly, "Way to go, Bethany!"

"Good job," Alicia said encouragingly.

Nathan nodded his approval.

"Keep going," prompted Sarah.

Beaming, Bethany proudly presented her report as she stood calf-deep in garbage! Yes! Bethany was standing in our trashcan, reading her report, and smiling like there was no better place to be in the world.

I was teaching psychology to a blended class of eleventh and twelfth graders, and that day's topic was "shaping." "Shaping," I explained, "is reinforcing successive approximations." Thirty blank stares later I reminded my students of the children's game, "Hot or Cold." The closer the person who was "it" got to a hidden object, the more the other players said things like, "You are getting warm — warmer — you're getting hot — hotter — really hot — you're burning up!" I explained that "shaping is reinforcing a behavior as it gets closer and closer to a desired target behavior." After a few more details and examples, I was confident my students were ready to apply their *shaping* lesson.

Being the sweet girl that she was, Bethany volunteered to run a couple of errands for me. In the brief time she was gone, I quickly informed my students that I would be calling on Bethany to give her report first. Their job was to determine from where Bethany would speak, and then use *shaping* to get her there. Within moments a target behavior was chosen and a plan was formed.

Taking her place in front of the class, with her report in hand, Bethany began giving her report to the class. Seconds later, she was obviously aware of her peers. Not a single student was looking her way. Some slouched in their seats. Others put their heads down on their desks. And a few inconsiderately whispered to a neighbor. In her discomfort, Bethany began moving around a little behind the podium. The second she took a step in the direction of the garbage can, her peers began paying attention to her words. She took a few more steps toward the trashcan. Now her peers were sitting up straighter, looking at her, and seeming to lean in to hear her words. They began encouraging her as she stood next to the garbage can, saying phrases like:

"You know you want to try it."

"Nobody will care."

"There's nothing wrong with it."

According to our official timekeeper, it took fewer than four minutes for Bethany to lift her foot and place it over the trash. As she made the gesture, the class broke into great clapping, and Bethany took the garbage plunge. She finished her report from her trashy spot, as her peers assured her with words of affirmation.

With the last few minutes left for our class, the students shared their thoughts on how well the shaping experiment worked. Bethany giggled and explained she really didn't *want* to stand in the trash, but did it because she could tell it was what the class wanted.

Quite abruptly the light and fun atmosphere changed when I revealed their next class topic: Compare shaping and peer pressure. Briefly describe a time when shaping has led you or somebody you care about into a trashy place.

That next assignment and experiment provided a lesson for a lifetime — even for the teacher!

* * *

Do not be misled: "Bad company corrupts good behavior."

1 CORINTHIANS 15:33

custodial care

Vicki Caruana

....

*You cannot be friends upon any other terms
than upon the terms of equality.*

WOODROW WILSON

J have the unique advantage as a teacher of knowing
what life is like for some of the most important staff
members in a school. My mother worked in food
services for seventeen years. My father worked in maintenance
as a plumber for our school district. The frustrations they dealt
with and the daily struggles they endured would sound familiar
to any teacher. Unfortunately, we don't spend much time talking to our lunch ladies or custodians, so we don't really know
what their days are like. But I do, and now so will you.

In one of the schools where I taught, the head custodian's
name was Frank. I learned, at my mother's apron, that it was
important that Frank and I become friends. After all, if we
weren't friends — or even worse, enemies — my classroom

would never get cleaned, we'd never get the things we needed, and I'd have to move heavy furniture all by myself. I knew that a good relationship with the custodial staff was one of the keys to a great school year.

But Frank wasn't easy to get close to. Maybe he had a sense that teachers were only nice to him in order to get what they wanted. Maybe he'd experienced a false sense of friendship in the past. He held me at arm's length, and my attempts at conversation were usually stifled. I didn't know what to do, and I began to question my motives. Maybe it wasn't right to befriend someone just in the hope that they could help you later on. In fact, when I said it out loud, it sounded terrible! I decided not to try so hard and to do what I could to foster a positive relationship with Frank whether he was helpful to me or not.

According to custodians, teachers are known not by the company they keep but by the classroom they keep. We're told to make sure that the chairs are stacked on top of the desks at the end of the day. If they're not, you can't complain the next day that your room wasn't vacuumed the night before. Even though custodians are there to clean up our messes, they have an entire school to do in a short period of time. We can be helpful by doing more than stack chairs.

These are some of the things I did that finally turned frowning Frank into fantastic Frank, the Frank who, on my last day of work before I had my first child, was the only one to walk me out and give me a proper good-bye. I had my students pick up every piece of paper or trash on the floor before they left each day (so that vacuuming would be more efficient). They also erased the boards and banged out the erasers (so the boards and erasers would get washed each night). We all made sure that bookcases were neatly arranged with no stray books left lying around (so the shelves could be dusted). I made sure my desk was neat and clear (so its surface would get wiped). And when we did a particularly messy activity or project, I cleaned up *everything* myself.

One day I had to leave early for a doctor's appointment, and I knew the substitute wouldn't leave my room as clean as she should. But the next morning I was surprised to find it clean as a whistle. I knew it was because of Frank. Early the next day I ventured down to where the custodians gathered, behind the boiler room, underneath the stairs, and presented his crew with a batch of homemade double chocolate brownies and a note of thanks.

It made Frank smile. We had many more conversations after that in the hallway and between classes. Our friendship grew genuinely over the next few years — and my classroom was always clean!

. . . .

Two people can accomplish more than twice as much as one; they get a better return for their labor. If one person falls, the other can reach out and help. But people who are alone when they fall are in real trouble.

Ecclesiastes 4:9 – 10 NLT

toads and diamonds

Bonnie Afman Emmorey

....

Kind words can be short and easy to speak;
their echoes are truly endless.

MOTHER TERESA

*I*t was Monday morning — and I was in trouble. I was looking at an extended time of substitute teaching in the local middle school. Many teachers try to avoid that age group all together, but that wasn't true for me. I usually loved it. The students were full of life and energy — old enough to learn and yet young enough to still get excited about what I was teaching.

But this was not going to be my normal middle school fare. I was scheduled to substitute in the EI classroom (emotionally impaired students). These were the tough kids. They were emotionally scarred and hurting, ready to lash out at *any* provocation. I was nervous before I arrived, and by the end of that first day, I knew that I was in over my head. These students were determined to make me sorry I ever thought I could teach. It was an exhausting day, and I was discouraged to the core.

That night insomnia pushed the counting of sheep from my brain, but somehow a *toad* slipped into my thoughts. As I was pleading with God for a creative way to deal with these disturbed children, an old French folk tale came to mind — "Toads and Diamonds." It was one of my favorites. My husband, Ron, also a teacher, introduced me to the wonderful world of folk tales early in our marriage. If I ever had trouble sleeping, he would read to me with his beautiful deep voice, and I would quickly drift into sleep.

"Toads and Diamonds" is the classic story of two stepsisters — one beautiful and good and the other ugly and nasty. The wonderful daughter took after her deceased father, and the horrible daughter was the spitting image of the equally nasty mother. The sweet daughter was forced daily to walk a mile to get water from the well, but she did it with a smile. One day an old woman was there and asked for a drink. The kind daughter gave it to her cheerfully. It turned out to be a good fairy, and she bestowed a gift upon the delightful girl. Every time she opened her mouth to speak, diamonds and precious stones would fall from her mouth.

When her stepmother saw the riches that were falling from her unloved daughter's mouth, she determined to send her favorite daughter to the well to gain the same gift. The ugly, nasty daughter complained bitterly, but the mother forced her to go, prepared to serve the old woman fairy and thus gain the *gift*. But there was no old woman at the well. There was a beautiful young woman in need of a drink. Not realizing that it was actually the same fairy, the nasty girl yelled at her to get her own drink if she was so thirsty. The fairy in response bestowed upon her the gift of toads and reptiles falling from her mouth every time she spoke.

Upon arriving home, the nasty girl spoke, and toads and snakes fell from her lips as she yelled at her mother and step-sister. The mother was so distressed and angry that she chased her unloved and beautiful stepdaughter into the woods and told her to never come home. Of course, the stepdaughter met a prince and he carried her away to his kingdom. The nasty girl became so unpleasant and uncomfortable to live with that her mother finally chased her away as well, and she went off into the woods and died.

I had an idea. My classroom was full of kids spewing forth toads and vipers every time they spoke. They were gifted at saying the meanest thing they could think to say. I determined to show them what they were doing by playing a "Toads and Diamonds" game. First I read the folk tale out loud to the class. They loved it! It was right up middle school thinking. Then I outlined the game. I started with a large bowl of M&M'S, aka "diamonds." Their goal was to have someone notice and comment back to me on their *good* behavior. Anytime I observed or got word back about their positive manner or speech, they were rewarded with a handful of M&M'S. When I saw something negative, or heard it from an outside source, the student got a toad — in this case a large X by his or her name on the board. If anyone acquired five Xs in one day, they were out of the game for the rest of the day.

They took to the game like true competitors. These students became the nicest, best-behaved kids in the school, and I had one of the most enriching experiences of my teaching years. Yes, many of them were on a sugar high by the end of the school day, but they *all* learned the value of evaluating what came out of their mouths.

* * *

A word aptly spoken is like apples of gold in settings of silver.

PROVERBS 25:11

parking lot pecking order

Vicki Caruana

. . . .

The art of being wise is the art of knowing what to overlook.

WILLIAM JAMES

*H*ave you ever found yourself singing "The Parking Lot Blues"? Parking in the faculty parking lot can be treacherous. If you're new to a school, it can even be disturbingly combative! You know what I'm talking about. Although "where to park" is not included in your teacher handbook, there are rules just the same. Often you don't find out what the rules are until you inadvertently break them.

There is a sort of hierarchy to who parks where. Understandably, the principal, assistant principal, and school secretary get the premium spots. You could assume that every other spot is up for grabs. You know what they say — *never assume*.

At one of my first schools, the portion of the parking lot that was paved was not large enough for all the cars, so many of us had to park out in the dirt. I learned after the first couple of days that if I wanted to park my brand-new car on asphalt, I would have to arrive a little earlier. Florida falls are wet. Dirt parking lots turn to mud. I wanted to keep myself as dry as possible and my car as mud free as possible.

The next day I did arrive early. There were plenty of paved spots from which to choose. I had an inkling that taking a spot close to the building might not be prudent, so I chose a less noticeable spot in the middle of the lot. My choice was noticed.

I first heard the grumbling in the teachers' lounge before first bell. Most of these teachers didn't know who I was yet, and I was grateful for the anonymity. Later, while my students were in gym class, one of my only friends steered me by the elbow into her classroom.

"Where did you park today?"

"In the lot," I said. "I got here early."

My friend's face fell. This was not welcome news.

"You can't just park anywhere!" She looked out her classroom window to see if anyone could see her talking to me.

"There aren't assigned spots, are there?"

"Well, not on paper or anything. But as a new teacher here, you need to park in the dirt."

She escorted me to the door and quickly disappeared back into her room. I was left standing in the hall wondering what I should do next.

Maybe I was chicken. Maybe I was naïve. I admit that I'm easily intimidated. I aim to please.

So during lunch I moved my car out into the dirt.

. . . .

I charge you, in the sight of God and Christ Jesus and the elect angels, to keep these instructions without partiality, and to do nothing out of favoritism.

1 TIMOTHY 5:21

classroom seasoning

Annetta E. Dellinger

....

One who is filled with joy preaches without preaching.

MOTHER TERESA

a saltshaker and a small flashlight could always be found on the desk in my mother's classroom. The unlikely pair was quite conspicuous, unless they were covered with papers. Those two items remained on her desk during the entire forty years of her teaching career. Whenever I would ask why, she would smile and say they made a difference in the way she taught.

Mother referred to her students as "my kids." She loved them and was passionate about being a good educator. I caught her contagious enthusiasm for teaching, and my childhood was consumed with playing school. My dolls and teddy bears were my pupils — I even made report cards for my students, and I disciplined them when they misbehaved.

Years later, when I signed my first contract to teach, my mother presented me with two special gifts and this letter:

To My Daughter,

What a great God we have! I praise him that I have lived long enough to see you become a teacher and make a difference in the lives of your students as his salt and light! Keep this old saltshaker on your desk. May it be a reminder that Jesus has called you to this classroom to make a difference for him. Let your conversations be full of grace, seasoned with salt. Don't be pressured to blend in with everyone else. Follow his spirit and affect others positively, just as seasoning brings out the best flavor in food!

The flashlight is to remind you to read the Bible daily. Immerse yourself in his strength-sustaining word, because he has chosen you to be his light to the children you are teaching. Let your "difference-maker-light" shine through the way you talk, teach, tackle challenges, and survive stress!

Carry the joy you have from your personal relationship with Jesus Christ into the atmosphere of your classroom, so others will be drawn to him!

Love,
Your Mother

P.S. I hope you have as much fun as I did when people ask about the salt and light on your desk!

Mother was right. Notes from former students and conversations with their parents affirm the difference a Christian influence brought to my classroom. My mother's advice, complete with two powerful visual aids, has made a positive difference in the way I teach!

. . . .

Let me tell you why you are here. You're here to be salt-seasoning that brings out the God-flavors of this earth. If you lose your saltiness, how will people taste godliness? . . . You're here to be light, bringing out the God-colors in the world. God is not a secret to be kept. We're going public with this, as public as a city on a hill. If I make you light-bearers, you don't think I'm going to hide you under a bucket, do you? I'm putting you on a light stand. Now that I've put you there on a hilltop, on a light stand — shine! Keep open house; be generous with your lives. By opening up to others, you'll prompt people to open up with God, this generous Father in heaven.

MATTHEW 5:13–16 MSG

wouldn't it be nice if . . . ?

Vicki Caruana

....

*Cleaning up "accidents" in the classroom
wasn't in the job description.*

KIMBERLY CHAMBERS

*I*t's good to dream. As teachers we tend to live so
much in the reality of the lives of our students that
we forget how to dream. Encouraging people to
dream gives them permission to make those dreams come true.
I remember one such dream session right before the beginning
of the school year.

"Wouldn't it be nice if . . . ?" I started.

It took a few moments before anyone would answer.

"Wouldn't it be nice if we had more technology than we
knew what to do with?"

"Wouldn't it be nice if the parents of our most struggling
students showed up for conferences?"

"Wouldn't it be nice if our salary increases kept up with the
cost of living?" This one got a laugh, even though the comment
was completely serious.

"Wouldn't it be nice if each teacher had no more than fifteen students?"

"Wouldn't it be nice if America appreciated her teachers?"

The mood was turning sullen. One of the teachers decided it was time to lighten things up a bit (she must have been a class clown in her school days).

"Wouldn't it be nice if everyone cleaned up their own vomit?"

We were all stunned into silence and for a moment that last word hung in the air.

I had to ask, "The teachers' or the students'?"

Everyone broke into relieved laughter and began to recall the days when a student got sick in the hall and another teacher had to clean it up. I guess this is something that happens more often in elementary schools, because I don't ever remember being responsible for such a task when I taught in the middle school.

Soon teachers actually came up with some incredible ideas to turn our school into our dream school. The encouraging thing was that we realized that many of our ideas were attainable. Becoming more a part of the decision-making process, having early release on Fridays, looking for ways to toot another teacher's horn could actually happen if we worked together.

Now it was just a matter of turning dreams into reality. Daydreaming was for once a worthwhile school activity. And I'm fairly certain that cleaning up your own vomit remains on the top ten ideas list!

. . . .

Forget the former things; do not dwell on the past. See, I am doing a new thing! Now it springs up; do you not perceive it?

ISAIAH 43:18–19

class picture day

Vicki Caruana

. . . .

Though we travel the world over to find the beautiful,
we must carry it with us or we find it not.

EMERSON

*O*nly people who actually like school become teachers. I know that may seem hard to imagine about
some teachers, but it's true. I loved everything about
going to school — except the annual school photo. I didn't mind
the class photo because I could only be seen from a distance. To
this day, I cringe at the thought of a posed-for photograph.

The problem with school photos, especially for teachers, is
that the student-teacher ratio is such that you are more apt to
notice a bad teacher photo than a bad student photo. So if I
had a bad hair day on picture day, I wasn't the only one who
noticed.

If you are not naturally photogenic, then picture day can
be a nightmare. For one thing, finding an inch of comfortable
space on those little stools is a challenge. Turning your head

this way and that and pointing your knees in the opposite direction takes the work of a contortionist (especially the older you get). And I'm never quite sure if I'm supposed to look at the camera lens or look at the blinking light above it. If you look at my yearbooks over the years, you'll know which years I guessed right and which I didn't.

Why can't school photos be like Glamour Shots? Why is it that only seniors in high school get their adolescent faces touched up? Some of us still deal with acne! I know it's a budget issue (isn't everything?), but think about days gone by. I've seen the photos of the teachers from the 1940s, '50s, and even '60s. You could tell that some were shot through cheesecloth. Color was lightly painted into the cheeks of the pale faced. Everyone had even skin tone!

So each year I enter the makeshift photographer's studio in the cafeteria with trepidation. I try to put my best face forward, sit on the tail of my jacket so it doesn't ride up, and smile with only a few teeth showing (the top two in the center are chipped from a gym accident when I was in third grade) and hope for the best. I'm just as anxious to get the pictures back. I don't even know why they give them to us. I have yet to send wallets of myself as a teacher to anyone in my family. You know it's more than a bad hair day when your school photo looks worse than your driver's license photo!

I have to remind myself that my focus and my desire need not be on either my appearance or my reputation. It's God's reputation and his countenance that make me attractive to others.

....

One thing I ask of the Lord, this is what I seek: that I may dwell in the house of the Lord all the days of my life, to gaze upon the beauty of the Lord and to seek him in his temple.

PSALM 27:4

teacher talk

Vicki Caruana

* *

Inspired teachers . . . cannot be ordered by the gross from the factory. They must be discovered one by one.

JOHN JAY CHAPMAN

*J*anet was grateful that spring break was finally here. It was time to indulge in her only passion — scrapbooking! She had signed up for a twenty-four–hour crop in her city at a hotel that catered every meal. As she settled in with her supplies at her table, she tried to forget about teaching and focus instead on her family photos.

"Did I give you copies of my photos from the planetarium field trip?" asked a voice from the table behind Janet.

"No," another voice said. "Do you have them with you? I'm running out of photos."

"Look at this one. See how surprised the kids looked when they saw the sphere from the outside?"

Janet's attention shifted from her Christmas photos to the table behind her. Were they teachers? The phrase *field trip* was a red flag. Maybe they were parents who chaperoned.

"I'm amazed we actually pulled off that field trip," the first voice continued.

"I know what you mean," said the second. "Getting enough parents to drive into the city was no easy task."

Oh, no! They're teachers! Janet felt as if the large hotel conference room was closing in on her. Maybe that would be the end of the conversation. Maybe they would get distracted by something important — like their own families. Her CD player and headphones were in the car. She thought about getting them before it was too late.

It was too late.

"Excuse me," said a woman sitting across from Janet. "You're a teacher too, aren't you?"

Too? How could she know such a thing? What was she — a mind reader? Janet thought about lying, but before she could even conceive of what profession she would say she was in, the woman said, "Your supplies are in a teacher bag. Looks like your school goes all out for their teachers."

Janet looked at her canvas bag. "Yes, I'm a teacher." This was going to be a long night.

Just then the coordinator came by to check on their progress.

"How's it going over here?" she said, looking directly at Janet. "Everyone acquainted? I put all you teachers together for the day. Won't that be fun?"

Everyone, all eight of them, squealed in delight, except Janet. Her frozen stare must have worried them because suddenly they were all asking her questions. She knew where this exchange would lead. First you compare notes. Then you jump right into complaining, and then finally into commiserating. Janet just wasn't up to it.

Where do you teach? How long have you been teaching? Is your school overcrowded too? Can you believe they turned down our raise request again? And then the conversations broke into more intimate groupings and all Janet could do was eye the exit door. She wondered if she could get her money back. She felt a panic attack building inside and wanted desperately to run out that door and into the seclusion of her faded blue Volvo.

Then a small voice broke into her thoughts. "Janet, I mean, Mrs. Bell. My name is Nicki Campbell. I wonder if you remember me."

Janet wasn't sure about the name, but those big, sparkling blue eyes were familiar. They belonged to a girl who rarely spoke in her class, but whose eyes followed Janet wherever she was in the room.

"Nicki, yes, I remember you." What was she doing here?

"I'm a teacher now, Mrs. Bell. When Debby told me the names of the other teachers coming to this crop, I was so excited to hear yours." Nicki pulled out the chair next to Janet and sat down. Janet didn't mind.

"A teacher? How wonderful." Janet's face softened and her thoughts of flight vanished.

"Because of you, Mrs. Bell. I'm a teacher because of you."

The next twenty-two hours flew by. Janet and Nicki talked about teaching, about learning, and about how they still wanted to make a difference in this world. By the end of the crop, Janet felt rejuvenated and proud to be called a teacher.

What we say out loud about teaching reflects what's in our hearts. Our words should be a help and never a hindrance to the journey of other teachers — especially beginning teachers. Let your words about teaching build up the profession and not cause those in it to stumble.

. . . .

Do not cause anyone to stumble, whether Jews,
Greeks or the church of God.

1 CORINTHIANS 10:32

the day the student became the teacher

Carole Brewer

. . . .

It's always helpful to learn from your mistakes because then your mistakes seem worthwhile.

GARRY MARSHALL

*J*t was five minutes before the hour and thirty-six fifth graders were lined up along the windows just outside the library. Their teacher eagerly looked in my direction for my okay to release her for her preparation period. At the same time, the thirty-six first graders I'd just finished teaching were lined up inside the library awaiting the arrival of their classroom teacher for pickup. She was a few minutes late and my bladder was full! I enjoyed my job as music appreciation teacher at Camellia Basic School, but there were days when my grueling schedule was challenging.

As the first grade class filed out, I asked the fifth grade teacher if she would please bring her class in and seat them, while I made a mad dash for the restroom. She agreed and I ran for it.

Three minutes later I was facing another group of students who were eagerly awaiting great nuggets of musical truth I was going to impart to them. Well, that's what I *wished* they were thinking.

As I opened my lesson planner, picked up the chalk, and started expounding on the topic of the day, sweet, shy Nicole, who was sitting in the very back of the room, raised her hand. I responded, "Not now, Nicole. I'll get to your question later."

Nicole's hand went up again. "Not now, Nicole," I said, but her hand stayed up. "Nicole, *wait*," I responded with exasperation.

To my amazement, my usually well-mannered, shy student stood up and started walking toward me. "What are you doing? Nicole, *sit down!*" I ordered in an exasperated tone.

I was speechless as Nicole kept walking in my direction. Reaching the front of the classroom where I stood, she whispered in my ear, "Your zipper's down," and she fled back to her seat.

It was a moment to remember. Thanking her under my breath, I immediately faced the chalkboard and pulled up the zipper on the front of my slacks. I'm not sure which shade of purple my face was wearing when I turned back to the students, but I vividly recall the variety of smirks on the faces of those fifth grade boys.

Later, as I considered the unstoppable persistence of Nicole, I realized my student modeled the relentless pursuit of my heavenly Father. In the busyness of my teaching career, it's often easy to put off my personal time with him.

Not now.

Later.

Wait.

The choice is mine. Sometimes I make the time to be alone in his presence. But often I'm on the run, wondering how I can fit one more thing into my day. But even when I put him off, he persistently waits for me and invites me to come away with him.

* * *

Are you tired? Worn out? . . . Come to me. Get away with me and you'll recover your life. I'll show you how to take a real rest. Walk with me and work with me — watch how I do it. Learn the unforced rhythms of grace.

MATTHEW 11:28 – 29 MSG

why i can't teach younger than third grade

Vicki Caruana

. . . .

*A good teacher is one who helps you
become who you feel yourself to be.*

Julius Lester

I love young children. Growing up you could always
find me entertaining the "little ones" at family gath-
erings. I was a great babysitter. I had patience. I had
fun! To me this was an indicator that I would make a great mom
someday. And since I had planned to become a teacher from a
very young age, I believed that I was meant to teach in the primary grades.

I was wrong.

Although I love my own children and enjoyed them
tremendously when they were three, four, five, and six years
old, I discovered much to my surprise that I didn't enjoy teaching those ages at all. My decision to go into special education

opened me up to a world of children who were desperately struggling. Life was "bad" very early in their young lives. I remember one particular season of student teaching in which I served in a primary classroom for children with emotional disturbances. I cried every night over those little ones who seemed so lost. I knew then that if I were going to remain in special education, I needed to teach older kids.

My second red flag that I was not meant for the primary grades was when I taught as a long-term substitute in a kindergarten classroom. I had thirty-two students, no aide, and absolutely no idea five-year-olds could be so messy (this was before I had my own children). They were adorable! But they had the wiggles, they didn't all sleep at nap time, and they needed help — a lot of help. They needed help tying their shoes, getting their coats on and off, and putting a Band-Aid on a barely scratched finger. They couldn't count. They couldn't cut. And they couldn't color.

They were sweet. They gave me hugs. They gave me presents. But they also gave me pinkeye, strep throat, and a rash no one could explain. I never worked so hard in all my life. The energy it took just to clean up the room each day felt like another full-time job. You know it's bad when the teacher falls asleep during nap time and the children have to be the ones to wake her up!

I needed kids with some skills. They had to be able to read. They had to be able to write. They had to be able to get to the bathroom without having an accident! During a year of substituting before I landed my first teaching job, I experienced every grade level. I found out what I was good at. I discovered that I was a junior high teacher.

I know those kids have "attitude," but believe me, they have skills! I spent most of my teaching career teaching junior high. I don't regret one moment of it.

. . . .

*And God is able to make all grace abound to you,
so that in all things at all times, having all that you need,
you will abound in every good work.*

2 CORINTHIANS 9:8

letters from teddy

Elizabeth S. Ungar

Children are not born knowing the many opportunities that are theirs for the taking. Someone who does know must tell them.

RUTH HILL VIGUERS

*a*n introduction to a much-loved story:

When a friend of Elizabeth S. Ungar told her about a boy who had brought his teacher a rhinestone bracelet with stones missing and a used bottle of perfume, she recalled the year her mother told her they would have to limit their gift giving due to family financial challenges. She couldn't bear the thought of not giving her fourth grade teacher, Mrs. Clinard, a Christmas present so she presented her with a cigar box filled with pecans that had fallen from her grandmother's trees.

Her classmates snickered and made unkind comments as Mrs. Clinard unwrapped the box of pecans. However, the teacher clapped her hands and said, "Oh, thank you so much, Elizabeth! I have company coming for Christmas and I need these pecans for my fruitcakes!" The teacher's enthusiastic response made Elizabeth feel valued.

Her recollection inspired her to write this story. The author has received more mail and phone calls on this story than anything else she has ever written. It's a gentle reminder of why we do what we do.

. . . .

Her name was Mrs. Thompson. As she stood in front of her fifth grade class on the very first day of school, she told the children a lie. Like most teachers, she looked at her students and said that she loved them all the same. But that was impossible, because there in the front row, slumped in his seat, was a little boy named Teddy Stoddard.

Mrs. Thompson had watched Teddy the year before and noticed that he didn't play well with the other children, that his clothes were messy, and that he constantly needed a bath. And Teddy could be unpleasant. It got to the point where Mrs. Thompson would actually take delight in marking his papers with a broad red pen, making bold Xs and then putting a big F at the top of his papers.

At the school where Mrs. Thompson taught, she was required to review each child's past records and she put Teddy's off until last. However, when she reviewed his file, she was in for a surprise. Teddy's first grade teacher wrote, "Teddy is a bright child with a ready laugh. He does his work neatly and has good manners . . . he is a joy to be around." His second grade teacher wrote, "Teddy is an excellent student, well liked by his classmates, but he is troubled because his mother has a terminal illness and life at home must be a struggle." His third grade teacher wrote, "His mother's death had been hard on him. He tries to do his best, but his father doesn't show much interest and his home life will soon affect him if some steps aren't taken." Teddy's fourth grade teacher wrote, "Teddy is withdrawn and doesn't show much interest in school. He doesn't have many friends and he sometimes sleeps in class."

By now, Mrs. Thompson realized the problem and she was ashamed of herself. She felt even worse when her students brought her Christmas presents, wrapped in beautiful ribbons and bright paper, except for Teddy's. His present was clumsily wrapped in the heavy brown paper that he got from a grocery bag. Mrs. Thompson took pains to open it in the middle of the other presents. Some of the children started to laugh when she found a rhinestone bracelet with some of the stones missing and a bottle that was one quarter full of perfume. But she stifled the children's laughter when she exclaimed how pretty the bracelet was, put it on, and dabbed some of the perfume on her wrist. Teddy Stoddard stayed after school that day just long enough to say, "Mrs. Thompson, today you smelled just like my mom used to." After the children left she cried for at least an hour. On that very day, she quit teaching reading, and writing, and arithmetic. Instead, she began to teach children.

Mrs. Thompson paid particular attention to Teddy. As she worked with him, his mind seemed to come alive. The more she encouraged him, the faster he responded. By the end of the year, Teddy had become one of the smartest children in the class and, despite her lie that she would love all the children the same, Teddy became one of her "teacher's pets." A year later, she found a note under her door, from Teddy, telling her that she was still the best teacher he ever had in his whole life.

Six years went by before she got another note from Teddy. He then wrote that he had finished high school, third in his class, and she was still the best teacher he ever had in his whole life.

Four years after that, she got another letter, saying that while things had been tough at times, he'd stayed in school, had stuck with it, and would soon graduate from college with the highest of honors. He assured Mrs. Thompson that she was still the best and favorite teacher he ever had in his whole life.

Then four more years passed and yet another letter came. This time he explained that after he got his bachelor's degree, he decided to go a little further. The letter explained that she was still the best and favorite teacher he ever had. But now his name was a little longer — the letter was signed, Theodore F. Stoddard, M.D.

The story doesn't end there. You see, there was yet another letter that spring. Teddy said he'd met this girl and was going to be married. He explained that his father had died a couple of years ago and he was wondering if Mrs. Thompson might agree to sit in the place at the wedding that was usually reserved for the mother of the groom. Of course, Mrs. Thompson did. And guess what? She wore that bracelet, the one with several rhinestones missing. And she made sure she was wearing the perfume that Teddy remembered his mother wearing on their last Christmas together. They hugged each other and Dr. Stoddard whispered in Mrs. Thompson's ear, "Thank you, Mrs. Thompson, for believing in me. Thank you so much for making me feel important and showing me that I could make a difference." Mrs. Thompson, with tears in her eyes, whispered back, "Teddy, you have it all wrong. You were the one who taught me that I could make a difference. I didn't know how to teach until I met you."

Remember that wherever you go and whatever you do, you will have the opportunity to touch and/or change a person's outlook. Try to add sunshine to someone else's life each and every day.

. . . .

The Lord bless you and keep you; the Lord make his face shine upon you and be gracious to you; the Lord turn his face toward you and give you peace.

NUMBERS 6:24–26

About Carol Kent, General Editor

Carol Kent is a popular international public speaker best known for being dynamic, humorous, encouraging, and biblical. She is a former radio show cohost and has been a guest on numerous television and radio programs. She is the president of Speak Up Speaker Services, a Christian speakers' bureau, and the founder and director of Speak Up With Confidence seminars, a ministry committed to helping Christians develop their communication skills. She has also founded the nonprofit organization Speak Up for Hope, which benefits the families of incarcerated individuals. A member of the National Speakers Association, Carol is often scheduled more than a year in advance for keynote addresses at conferences and retreats throughout the United States and abroad.

She holds a master's degree in communication arts and a bachelor's degree in speech education. Her books include: *When I Lay My Isaac Down, Becoming a Woman of Influence, Mothers Have Angel Wings, Secret Longings of the Heart, Tame Your Fears, Speak Up With Confidence*, and *Detours, Tow Trucks, and Angels in Disguise*. She has also cowritten with Karen Lee-Thorp *My Soul's Journey* and the *Designed for Influence Bible Studies*. Carol has been featured on the cover of *Today's Christian Woman* and her articles have been published in a wide variety of magazines. To schedule Carol to speak for your event, call 888-870-7719 or contact her at *www.SpeakUp SpeakerServices.com* or *www.CarolKent.org*.

About Vicki Caruana

Vicki Caruana is the best-selling author of *Apples & Chalkdust*, which has sold more than 600,000 copies. Trademarked as "America's Teacher," she teaches teachers to evaluate the job they're doing, to encourage one another, and to be empowered with prayer. As an educational consultant, Vicki speaks at a variety of venues to reach kids and their parents. She speaks nationally at educational conferences, homeschool conventions, colleges, and schools, presenting workshops for teachers, parents, and kids. She also launched Teachers in Prayer, which teaches teachers how to pray through their daily dilemmas and struggles.

Vicki's books include: *Apples & Chalkdust — Inspirational Stories and Encouragement for Teachers, Giving Your Child the Excellence Edge, Apples of Gold for Teachers, The ABC's of Homeschooling, Apples & Chalkdust #2 — More Inspirational Stories and Encouragement for Teachers,* and *The Organized Homeschooler.* She has written on educational issues for publications such as *Christian Parenting Today, Homeschooling Today, Focus on the Family, Our Children,* and *Highlights for Children.*

Vicki is available for keynotes and for workshops for both teachers and students. To schedule her to speak for your event, call 888-870-7719 or contact her at www.applesandchalkdust.com or www.SpeakUp SpeakerServices.com.

Contributors

Karen Allaman lives in western Pennsylvania. She holds a master's degree in elementary education and is a certified reading specialist. She has taught elementary school for nineteen years. Karen also speaks at women's events and conferences. For additional information, email Karen at rallaman@csonline.net.

Carole Brewer is a recording artist, minister in song, and a popular speaker at women's conferences and retreats. Carole has been featured on many Christian television and radio programs and has produced four music CDs: *Celebrate the Lord, Everything Began With You, New Life,* and *The Work of Your Hand.* She also shares her expertise as a vocal coach in her book titled *Cookin' Up a Song* and in her voice-training seminars. For information, visit her website at www.carolebrewer.com.

Judith Conger, a public school teacher for thirty-seven years, is now retired and pursuing another career — that of serving others through her interests in writing, sewing, and painting. Her writing collection includes poetry, short stories, and manuscripts for young children and middle readers. She finds the greatest benefit to be self-healing through God's gift of words.

Annetta E. Dellinger is known as "The Joy Lady." She is founder and president of Joyful Ministries and a speaker with Speak Up Speaker Services. She is author of thirty books, including *Be Joyful . . . Who Me? Mini Joy-Spirations to Energize Your Day.* For information, contact Annetta at www.Annettadellinger.com. To schedule Annetta for a speaking engagement, call 888-870-7719.

Jennie Afman Dimkoff is the president of Storyline Ministries Inc. and is the author of *Night Whispers: Bedtime Bible Stories for Women*, and *More Night Whispers: Bedtime Bible Stories for Women*. Jennie travels nationally as a keynote speaker and is also a speaker-trainer with Speak Up With Confidence seminars. For additional information, go to www.JennieAfmanDimkoff.com. To schedule Jennie as a speaker, call 888-870-7719.

Bonnie Afman Emmorey is a speaker consultant with Speak Up Speaker Services, teaches communication skills for Speak Up With Confidence seminars, and is helping to launch Speak Up with Hope. For information, go to www.SpeakUpForHope.org and www.SpeakUp SpeakerServices.com.

Janet Fleck has been a principal for fifteen years. She taught junior high school and elementary school for seventeen years before becoming a principal. Janet received her bachelor of science degree and teaching certificate from Spring Arbor University and earned her master's degree in educational leadership from Oakland University. Janet is grateful to Cathy Gallagher for writing her stories that appear in this book.

Cathy Gallagher has been a salesperson, marketing manager, customer service director, assistant dean, and president of her own speaking and writing business. She has authored numerous articles for business publications and has ghostwritten a book on business communications. She is actively involved in a prayer ministry and a prison ministry through her church. Cathy speaks and writes on a wide variety of subjects. Contact Cathy to speak for your group by calling 888-870-7719.

Kim Stafford-Galaviz is a wife and mother of three girls. She is a middle school English and art teacher and enjoys writing, scrapbooking, and decoupage. Kim has published several poems, newspaper articles, and a workbook on poetry. Her most recent accomplishment is helping her husband, Rob, graduate from college.

Phyllis Olay Harmony is the president of Speaking in Harmony and has contributed to five books of inspirational poetry by her mother, Louise Thompson, as a writer and illustrator. She travels nationally as a keynote speaker, and her goal is to help audiences find their humble significance as a child of God. To schedule Phyllis for your next event, go to www.speakinginharmony.com.

Cynthia Spell Humbert was a Christian counselor at the prestigious Minirth-Meier Clinic in Dallas, Texas, for seven years and a frequent guest speaker on the clinic's national radio program. She has earned master's degrees in counseling psychology and Christian counseling. She is the author of *Deceived by Shame, Desired by God* and a contributor to many other books. Several of her stories have been published by Honor Books and Beacon Hill Press. Cynthia travels nationally as a keynote speaker for women's conferences and marriage retreats. To schedule Cynthia as a speaker for your next event, call 888-870-7719.

Bernadine Johnson is grateful God has given her the gifts of being a wife, mother, grandmother, teacher, and musician. Since graduating from Indiana Wesleyan University, she has been teaching piano, adjudicating, writing, and performing. Bernadine is published with Alfred Publishing, FJH Music Company, Word Publishing, Benson, and Lillenas. She believes every music student is unique and each person should be given time, respect, acceptance, opportunity, and music that inspires them to continue the journey.

Melissa S. Sutter lives in Grant, Michigan, with her husband and her two sons. A graduate of Central Michigan University, Melissa earned her degree in secondary education with a major in psychology and minors in math and computer science. She taught high school for eleven years. Currently Melissa is the principal at Grant Christian School. She is also the Coffee Break director at a nearby church and co-leads the Caring Ministry team and leads the Women's Ministry team at Bailey Christian Church. Melissa writes short stories, skits, and organizational tips and tools for Coffee Breaks. She has been published in *Encounters with God*.

Elizabeth S. Ungar is the mother of two grown children and grandmother to three. "The Teddy Story" is included in the book *Three Letters from Teddy and Other Stories*. Elizabeth, along with her sister and mother, coauthored the book *Whooppin' and Hollerin' in Onslow County*. She works for the Department of Social Services, is an avid reader, and enjoys sewing and playing the organ. Contact her at Elizabeth.Ungar@dss.virginia.gov.

Jeanne Zornes is a women's retreat and conference speaker, and the author of hundreds of articles and seven books, including *When I Prayed for Patience . . . God Let Me Have It!* She lives in Washington State. Contact her at P.O. Box 4362, Wenatchee, WA 98807-4392.

kisses of sunshine

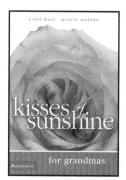

Hardcover
0-310-24766-7

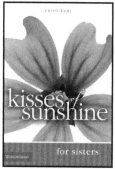

Hardcover
0-310-24846-9

Hardcover
0-310-24765-9

Hardcover
0-310-24767-5

Hardcover
0-310-24768-3

Pick up a copy today at your favorite bookstore!

ZONDERVAN™

GRAND RAPIDS, MICHIGAN 49530 USA

WWW.ZONDERVAN.COM